100 GREATEST U.S. COINS

by Jeff Garrett and Ron Guth

ACKNOWLEDGEMENTS

SPECIAL CREDIT TO TOM MULVANEY AND MICHAEL BERKMAN

David Akers	John Hamrick
Q. David Bowers	Larry Hanks
John Dannreuther	Robert Harwell
Richard Doty	Robert Lecce
Charles Ellis	Douglas Mudd
Mary Lynn Garrett	Harvey Stack
Maggie Guth	Doug Winter

Correspondence concerning this book's contents should be directed to the publisher:

H.E. Harris & Co.®
Serving the Collector Since 1916

3101 Clairmont Road
Suite C
Atlanta, Georgia 30329
www.heharris.com

Copyright © 2003 H.E. Harris & Co., Atlanta, GA
ISBN: 0-7948-1665-7

Art Direction: Matthew W. Jeffirs
Book Design: Robert A. Cashatt
Editor: Teresa Lyle

Printed in Italy

TABLE OF CONTENTS

THE GREATEST 100 U.S. COINS

TABLE OF CONTENTS

FOREWORD

Although many adjectives can be applied to rare coins, one word that never goes out of style is this: interesting. A coin may have a certain weight, certain diameter, certain market value, and certain grade, but no one of these on its own can explain why generations of Americans and others have desired rare coins over such a long period of time and have enjoyed owning them.

My congratulations go to Ron Guth and Jeff Garrett for conducting a survey among dealers as to which coins, primarily classic scarcities and rarities, have been in the limelight during the past generation. As will be seen on the pages to follow, the results range from the expected to the obscure, but in each instance, each coin is basically interesting to contemplate.

From the cradle days of American numismatics in the mid-nineteenth century, to the early twenty-first century, the 1804 dollar, not at all the rarest of all coins, has captured the lion's share of fame. Although there have been exceptions now and then, it is a handy rule of thumb that at any given time in the marketplace for the past 150 years, the highest price paid for any United States coin has been for the 1804 dollar. The Chapman brothers generations ago called the 1804 the "King of the United States Coins," a handy title that was amplified by B. Max Mehl and many others since.

Similarly, the 1913 Liberty Head nickel is the stuff of which numismatic dreams are made, and it comes in for its share of attention on the following pages. Then there is the fascinating, popular, rare, but also very available (thousands of examples exist of each) 1856 Flying Eagle Cent and MCMVII (1907) High Relief Double Eagle. Beyond that, an even more popular and available coin is the 1909-S V.D.B. Cent, a coin that every school kid hoped to find in pocket change 50 years ago.

A beautiful part of numismatics is that a coin can be worth 1 point, history can be worth another 1 point, rarity can be another 1 point, and value still another 1 point, yielding 1+1+1+1, which, per Albert Einstein, might equal 4, but which numismatists know might equal 10 or more. The whole is worth more than the sum of its parts!

How fortunate it is that we can read the history of 100 classics in this book. And beyond that, each coin has its special secrets: who has owned it, where it has been. While a few classics are thoroughly documented in this regard, most are not. Thus, if you buy a 1909-S V.D.B. Cent, you can gaze upon it wistfully and contemplate what it might say if it could only speak!

No reader of this present volume will ever obtain one of every coin listed here. It is impossible. Similarly, no reader of a catalog of paintings will acquire all of the top examples of Rembrandt, Picasso, DaVinci, and other masters from medieval times to the present.

A feasible alternative, and a very enjoyable one via the book you now hold, is to read about such treasures of art, numismatics, architecture, natural history, or of any other specialty. The authors have done a fine job of collecting a diverse series of rarities, bringing together essential information in a handy form that will no doubt be consulted again and again. In each instance, whatever aura a particular coin possessed to merit listing in this "Top 100" will be further enhanced by the publication of this great book.

Q. David Bowers
Wolfeboro, NH

WHAT IS THE GREATEST U.S. COIN?

One of the first questions new collectors ask is: "What is the greatest U.S. coin?"

The answer to that question is not as simple as one might think. Because we all come from different backgrounds and our experiences in numismatics are different, our answers to the question will also be different. For example, the person who has collected Lincoln Head Cents will probably choose one of the rare dates in that series, perhaps the one coin he or she still needs to complete the set – because, to that collector, that is the greatest coin. Another person might choose the most valuable coin–or the rarest coin–or the coin with the most beautiful design.

WHAT MAKES A COIN GREAT?

Greatness is subjective. Much of "greatness" depends on personal tastes and preferences. However, greatness also depends on objective factors, characteristics that can be measured against each other and from one coin to another. All of the great coins listed in this book will have one or more of the following characteristics:

Rarity – great coins are rare, meaning that only a few were made or, in some instances, only a few survived. Many of the coins in this book are unique; others are so rare that they are almost impossible to obtain because they come to market so infrequently. However, others are rare in the context of their series, and for some "popular rarities," such as the 1909-S V.D.B. Lincoln Cent, tens of thousands survive.

Value – great coins are generally expensive, but not necessarily so. The 1787 Fugio Cent (available in Choice Uncirculated condition for under $3,000), ranks right above the 1861 Paquet Reverse $20 gold piece (worth 100 times as much)!

Quality – great coins are usually in exceptional condition. However, high quality does not necessarily mean perfection. For example, the finest 1802 Half Dime is only About Uncirculated.

Popularity – great coins are appreciated by a large audience. Some coins may be rare and valuable, but the voting for the Top Hundred Coins illustrated how much of a popularity contest this really was. Why else would the 1909-S VDB Cent, of which thousands exist, rank a full ten places higher than the unique 1870-S Half Dime?

Beauty – great coins are aesthetically pleasing. For example, part of the allure of the 1872 Amazonian Gold Pattern set (#11 on the Top 100 list) is the sheer beauty and uniformity of the designs and the soft, mellow color of the gold in which they were struck.

History – great coins have a story to tell. Who can resist the incredible story of the 1804 Silver Dollars (#1 on the list), how they were first made in 1834, how some of them traveled from the Far East to Europe and back to America? Or the fascinating history behind the 1792 Silver-Center Cent and how the early Mint worked so hard to produce new coins for a new country.

CHOOSING AMERICA'S 100 GREATEST COINS

Picking the 100 Greatest American Coins was no easy task. The problem: too many great American coins. By restricting ourselves to 100 coins, we were forced to exclude some promising candidates or combine some in order to make room for others. For instance, instead of describing all four date and design combinations of the $4 Gold "Stellas" separately, we chose to combine them together.

We also excluded any non-official U.S. coins. This left out most Colonial coins, all of the Confederate coins, and virtually all of the Territorial gold coins. Many major varieties made it onto the list, but obscure varieties did not. But, even with these necessary exclusions, we believe the list we developed will satisfy the majority of collectors.

SO, HOW DID WE CHOOSE THE GREATEST AMERICAN COIN?

In this case, the decision was simple – we let someone else decide! We asked the members of the Professional Numismatists Guild (PNG), all leaders in the numismatic community, to vote on a list of the Top 100 Coins that we developed. We asked them to add any coins that they felt should have been included on the list. Most respondents ranked at least ten coins, but some ranked all 100! To choose the Top Ten coins, votes were weighted (a #1 vote was worth 10 points, a #2 vote was worth 9 points, and so on). The votes and their weighted scores were then tabulated. Because of the variety of responses received, the weighted scores provided a ranking for the Top 20 coins. We ranked the rest.

The voting produced some interesting results:

The top coin (the 1804 Silver Dollar) received twice as many #1 votes as any other coin. Its weighted score was 27% higher than the #2 coin. It seems that the so-called "King of American Coins" occupies its throne securely!

The #2 coin (the 1913 Liberty Head Nickel) received very few #1 votes, but it ranked so high on most people's vote sheets that the weighted score propelled it to the #2 spot.

The #7 coin (the 1907 Indian Head Pattern Double Eagle, Judd 1776) received the second highest number of #1 votes.

Neither the #9 coin (the 1822 Half Eagle) nor the #10 coin (the 1885 Trade Dollar) received a single #1 vote!

THE RESULTS: The Top 100 Greatest American Coins are presented in the following pages in rank order from the first coin to the 100th .
Whether you agree with the rankings or not, we hope you'll enjoy learning about these special coins. They are truly America's greatest coins.

The Professional Numismatists Guild was founded in 1955, and today is the leading numismatic society in the United States. Membership in the PNG was initially by invitation. Now a dealer may elect to join but must demonstrate that he or she brings expertise to the society and must be elected by a majority of members. The PNG is committed to educational outreach programs that benefit the numismatic industry and has hosted seminars and has sponsored scholarship essay contests to help educate the public about coins. For further information about this fine organization, visit **www.pngdealers.com**.

VOTING LIST

Last	First	Last	First	Last	First
Akers	David W.	Imhof	Todd L.	Rhue	Robert
Avena	Robert L.	Ivy	Steve	Roberts	Greg
Avena	Dan	Jones	Harry E.	Rodgers	Brad
Barnett	Loren D.	Kagin	Don	Rosen	Maurice
Berg	David	Ketterling	Don	Rowe	John N.
Berk	Harlan J.	Kutcher	Bruce	Schinke	Glenn
Bohnert	Brad	Laibstain	Harry	Scirpo	Anthony Michael
Bullowa	Mrs. C.E.	Lecce	Robert B.	Shafer	Leonard
Burd	William A	Lee	Larry L.	Simmons	Van
Campbell	Robert H.	Leidman	Julian M.	Spence	Larry Gerald
Casper	Michael	Leventhal	Edwin	Stack	Harvey
Dannreuther	John West	Levinson	Robert	Steinberg	Robert L.
Davisson	Allan	Lopresto	Samuel	Storeim	Michael R.
Degler	Klaus	McCawley	Chris Victor	Stuppler	Barry S.
Denley	Thomas M	Mercer	Daryl	Swiatek	Anthony J.
Donnelly	John	Miller	Wayne	Terranova	Anthony
Duncan	Kathleen	Mills	Warren T.	Van Grover	Jacob Jay
Edler	Joel T.	Munzner	Richard T.	Weinberg	Fred
Froseth	Kent Morris	Nachbar	Richard N.	Weitz	Harold B.
Goldberg	Lawrence S.	Napolitano	Chris	Whitlow	Larry
Goldberg	Ira M.	Noe	Thomas W.	Whitnah	Paul R.
Goldberg	Mark E.	Noxon	Casey	Williams	Dale L.
Greenberg	Frank	Olmstead	David	Winter	Douglas A.
Halperin	James L.	Pappacoda	Andrew	Woodside	John J.
Hamrick	John	Perlin	Joel D.	Wrubel	Gordon J.
Hanks	Larry	Pienta	Peter R.	Youngerman	William J.
Hendelson	Brian	Piret	Diane		
Henry	Gene L.	Ponterio	Richard H.		
Humphreys	George B	Ratner	Daniel N.		

1804 SILVER DOLLAR

The 1804 Silver Dollar was the clear winner in the voting for the Greatest American coin and deservedly so. For many years, the 1804 Silver Dollar was the most valuable United States coin (knocked from that perch only recently when the 1933 Double Eagle sold for $7.59 million). The 1804 Silver Dollar has received more press and publicity, and more has been written about it, than any other coin in the world. In fact, the 1804 Silver Dollar is the only coin to have been the subject of not one, but two, books. Eric Newman and Kenneth Bressett's *The Fantastic 1804 Silver Dollar* and Q. David Bowers *The Rare Silver Dollars Dated 1804 and the Exciting Adventures of Edmund Roberts*. 1804 Dollars have been on television, they've been the highlight displays at major coin conventions, and they are always the featured coins of any auction in which they appear. More importantly, they appear at the top of just about every collector and dealer's "wish list." When we tabulated the voting to determine the ranking of the Top 100 Greatest American coins, the 1804 Silver Dollar emerged as the clear winner, receiving 27% more votes than the #2 coin.

The story of the 1804 Silver Dollar begins in 1834, during the administration of Andrew Jackson, when the State Department ordered special sets of coins for presentation to the King of Siam and the Sultan of Muscat as diplomatic gifts. The Mint interpreted this to mean one coin of each legal denomination. However, the Silver Dollar and Eagle had not been made since 1804 (the Dollars reported in 1804 were actually dated 1803), so the Mint created new dies for each and struck a small number of coins for inclusion in the sets. Today, these are known as the "Original" (or Class I) 1804 Silver Dollars. Only eight Original 1804 Silver Dollars are currently traced.

Around 1858, a small number of 1804 Silver Dollars were struck using a different reverse die and lightweight planchets. One was struck over an 1857 Swiss Shooting Thaler (helping later researchers to unravel the mystery of the 1804 Silver Dollars). This batch is known as the "First Restrike" (or Class II) 1804 Silver Dollars. Because their edges were plain, they created an instant scandal when collectors first saw them, forcing their immediate recall and destruction. Only the overstrike on the 1857 Swiss coin has survived to represent the Class II variety (it now resides in the National Numismatic Collection at the Smithsonian Institution).

Having learned from their mistakes, the "minters" began using planchets of more or less proper weight and adding the appropriate lettering to the edges of the coins. These coins met with better success on the market and today six of these 1804 "Second Restrike" (or Class III) Silver Dollars are known.

All 1804 Silver Dollars share a common obverse die. The reverse die of the Class I 1804 Silver Dollars is different from that used on the Class II and Class III 1804 Silver Dollars. Only the Smithsonian Institution possesses examples of all three Classes!

Recent years have seen a flurry of appearances of the 1804 Silver Dollar, fueled perhaps by the huge prices they bring at auction. Since 1995 four different 1804 Silver Dollars have appeared at auction. In 1997, the Class I Stickney-Eliasberg example brought $1,815,000. In 1999, the Proof-68 Class I Watters-Childs example was sold by Bowers and Merena Galleries for a whopping $4,140,000, exceeding most expectations by at least a million or two dollars. In 2000, the Class I Dexter-Dunham example realized $1,840,000. Finally, the Class III Adams-Carter 1804 Silver Dollar sold for $874,000 in 2001. When another 1804 Silver Dollar will appear on the market is anyone's guess, but we suspect that the frequency will decrease. The coins sold in recent years have gone into strong hands, and the ones that were already "off the market" and in institutional collections will remain so.

Designed by Robert Scot. The obverse of each coin features a draped bust of Liberty with some of her hair tied back in a bow. LIBERTY appears above, the date below, and the stars are divided up on the sides (seven on the left, six on the right). The reverse of each coin features an heraldic eagle with outstretched wings (similar to that seen on the Great Seal of the United States). In its beak, the eagle holds a scroll with the words E PLURIBUS UNUM (One of many). In its left talon, the eagle grasps an olive branch; in its right talon, it holds a bunch of arrows. Clouds and 13 stars appear above the eagle. The outer legend reads: UNITED STATES OF AMERICA. No denomination appears anywhere on the coin. Standards: weight varies from 392 to 416 grains; composition .900 silver/.100 copper; diameter 39-40 mm. Edge: plain or lettered HUNDRED CENTS ONE DOLLAR OR UNIT.

Rarity: Extremely Rare. Only 15 1804 Silver Dollars are known, including eight Originals (Class I) and Restrikes (including one Class II and six Class III's). The finest example known is the amazing Proof-68 Watters-Childs example that set a then-record price of $4.14 million when it sold at auction in 1999.

Historical Value
Choice Proof
1960: $30,000 • 1980: $250,000 • 2003: $3,000,000

1804 SILVER DOLLAR

Photography courtesy Tom Mulvaney

Twenty years ago, if you asked any collector or dealer to name the three most valuable American coins, the response would most likely have been the following: 1804 Silver Dollar, 1894-S Dime, and 1913 Liberty Head Nickel. While the dynamics and rankings of the most valuable American coins have changed in the past decade, the 1913 Liberty Head Nickel is right up there near the top, currently tied at third most valuable.

The 1913 Liberty Head Nickel is a coin that simply should not exist. The Liberty Head Nickel series ended in December 1912, to be replaced in 1913 by the newly designed Buffalo Nickel. In fact, no 1913 Liberty Head Nickels were known or even contemplated until 1919, when Samuel Brown teased the collecting community by advertising to pay $500 for any 1913 Liberty Head Nickel. Apparently, this was just a ruse to legitimize coins that he already owned, for in August of 1920, Brown exhibited at least one of them at the annual convention of the American Numismatic Association. Brown eventually owned five (and possibly six) 1913 Liberty Head Nickels.

How did Brown obtain the coins? It may have helped that he was the Clerk of the Mint in 1912 and 1913, at which time he and confederates may have made the coins using Mint equipment.

The 1913 Liberty Head Nickels traded hands several times but remained together as a set until the early 1940s, when they were finally sold to individual buyers. Since then, the coins have taken widely divergent paths.

One went to King Farouk of Egypt, whose collection was sold in 1954 after he was deposed. His 1913 Liberty Head Nickel was casually added to a large collection of other nickels(!) and sold as part of a large lot. It went into the hands of Mrs. Emery May Holden Norweb, who ultimately donated the coin to the Smithsonian Institution.

A second example was sold to Louis Eliasberg (who formed the only complete collection of U.S. coins ever assembled). This coin, a superb Gem, is perhaps the finest of the known examples and is one of just two with full Proof surfaces, and it recently sold for $1.84 million.

The third example, a Choice Proof, has been viewed and owned by more people than any other. In 1972, this 1913 Liberty Head Nickel became the first American coin to break the $100,000 barrier. It later appeared in an episode of the TV program *Hawaii Five-O*, as the object of a crook's desire.

The fourth 1913 Liberty Head Nickel is most likely in the collection of a famous North Carolina family. Rumors that this coin spilled onto a highway and was lost in the traffic accident death of dealer George O. Walton are probably false, but the story is a good one.

The fifth example is a centerpiece of the American Numismatic Association's collection, having been donated some years ago by Aubrey and Adeline Bebee. The condition of this piece is significantly lower than the other 1913 Liberty Head Nickels because of the curious habits of the previous owner, James McDermott, who carried it as a pocket piece for bragging rights and betting purposes, sometimes passing it around to patrons gathered around a bar! By the time McDermott decided to protect his coin, it was worn down to EF grade.

A sixth piece was once rumored to exist because the five 1913 Liberty Head Nickels were once housed together in a six-hole case. The sixth coin turned out to be an electrotype bronze Pattern Buffalo Nickel, which conspiracy theorists speculate was substituted for the sixth 1913 Liberty Head Nickel!

Designed by Charles Barber. The obverse of the coin features a head of Liberty with her hair pulled up in a bun, wearing a wreath and a coronet inscribed with the word LIBERTY. The date appears below the head and 13 stars surround. On the reverse of the coin, a large "V" (the Roman numeral for "5") figures prominently in the center, surrounded by a wreath. A small E PLURIBUS UNUM appears in an arc above the "V" and a larger UNITED STATES OF AMERICA appears near the outer edge. The word CENTS appears beneath the wreath. Standards: weight 5 grams; composition .750 copper/.250 nickel; diameter 21 mm. Edge: plain.

Rarity: At present, the whereabouts of only four of the 1913 Liberty Head Nickels are known. The finest example is the Proof-66 Eliasberg example mentioned above.

Historical Value
Choice Proof
1960: $50,000 • 1980: $250,000 • 2003: $2,000,000

1913 LIBERTY HEAD NICKEL

Photography courtesy Numismatic Guaranty Corporation

The 1933 Double Eagle is one of the only coins to be a central figure in a U.S. government sting operation. In April 1933, the recently inaugurated President Franklin D. Roosevelt issued Executive Order 6102, instructing all American citizens to surrender their gold. Banks were prohibited from paying out gold coins or gold certificates. From March 15th until May 19th of 1933, the U.S. government struck a total of 445,000 Double Eagles. With the exception of two coins sent to the Smithsonian in 1934, it was thought that the remaining mintages of 1933 Double Eagles were melted in 1937. It is now certain that a small number of coins that had been set aside for assay purposes somehow escaped the Mint. To this day, the United States government claims that these coins were stolen and illegal to own. It is now believed by some that the first 1933 Double Eagle was sold privately in 1937 to James G. Macallister for $500. Over the next few years, nearly a dozen examples entered the marketplace. B. Max Mehl sold a 1933 Double Eagle to King Farouk of Egypt in February of 1944. In 1944, the collection of Colonel James W. Flanagan was offered at public auction by Stack's. In March, after having been alerted to the impending sale, Treasury agents confiscated the Flanagan specimen. No compensation was made, and it is believed that the coin was melted. Several others were also confiscated, and they are presumed melted. One collector, L.G. Barnard, fought the confiscation in court and lost. Private ownership of 1933 Double Eagles was officially deemed illegal.

In 1954, the ruling military junta in Egypt sold the King Farouk collection after the monarch had been overthrown. Farouk's 1933 Double Eagle was included. At the request of the U.S. government, the Egyptian government withdrew the coin from the sale. The Double Eagle then dropped from sight for nearly 50 years. In 1996, what was billed as the Farouk specimen, was secretly sold by a London dealer to American professional numismatists, in a New York City hotel room, for around one million dollars. The buyers, however, turned out to be government agents, and the coin was confiscated and the sellers were arrested. A legal battle ensued. Criminal charges were dropped and the ownership of the coin was fought for several years in court. The sellers were able to demonstrate that the U.S. government had issued export papers for the Farouk example. On January 25, 2001, just days before jury selection was to begin, both parties settled the case by agreeing to sell the coin and split the proceeds. The most interesting stipulation was that the alleged Farouk example would be the only 1933 Double Eagle considered legal to own. The United States government would officially monetize and issue this single 1933 Double Eagle. The auction of the coin was expected to bring between three and five million dollars, making it possibly the most valuable U.S. coin. The coin realized an astonishing seven and a half million dollars, a new record for any numismatic item. The buyer has yet to be identified.

Many may ask: "Why would someone pay over seven million dollars for a coin?" The most obvious answer is because they can! It must be remembered that in the same room in which the 1933 Double Eagle sold, paintings have been sold for close to one hundred million dollars. Jewelers regularly sell fine pieces for extraordinary sums. For the very rich, the pursuit of the finest or greatest of any field of interest is extremely alluring. Currently, only one person can publicly claim to own a 1933 Double Eagle. The coin's previous "forbidden fruit" status gives the piece incredible desirability. The 1933 Double Eagle is also the last coin in an extremely popular series. Only one individual can now own a complete set of Saint-Gaudens' Double Eagles.

The final chapter of this fascinating coin has not yet been written. It is almost certain that additional coins still survive and are privately held underground. Already the groundwork is being laid to challenge the government's claim that Double Eagles are illegal to own. Extensive research has been done on the story of the 1933 Double Eagle, and at least one book should be forthcoming. Look for this coin to continue making headlines for the foreseeable future!

Designed by Augustus Saint-Gaudens. The obverse depicts a standing Liberty draped in Romanesque clothing and holding a torch. The reverse features an eagle in a flying position. Mintage for this issue was 445,500, but nearly all examples were melted. Standards: weight 33.436 grams; composition .900 gold/.100 copper; diameter is 34 mm; net weight .96750 ounces of pure gold. Edge: lettered includes E PLURIBUS UNUM with the words divided by stars.

Rarity: Three examples are officially known to exist: two in the Smithsonian and the one referenced above. Four or five more are rumored to exist.

Historical Value
Choice Uncirculated
1960: $25,000 • 1980: $250,000 • 2003: $7,500,000

1933 DOUBLE EAGLE

Photography courtesy Smithsonian Institution and Douglas Mudd

Although technically a Pattern or experimental coin, the 1849 Double Eagle is nevertheless one of the great rarities of United States coinage. Following the discovery of gold in California in 1848, a tremendous flow of the yellow metal made its way to the East Coast. On March 3, 1849, federal legislation to create Gold Dollars and Double Eagles was enacted. The production of Double Eagles would convert the bullion into coins with the least effort.

Chief Engraver James B. Longacre engraved the dies for the new coinage. With great difficulty, Longacre supervised an attempt to strike the new denomination. In a letter dated December 24, 1849, from Franklin Peale, Chief Coiner, to Mint Director Robert Patterson, Peale wrote: "It is with extreme regret and after the most earnest endeavors to overcome the difficulty that I am compelled to inform you that the impression upon the new die, for the double eagle, cannot be brought up by the usual coining processes." The relief of the portrait was too high, and the coins could not be struck properly for mass production. These delays in production resulted in just a handful of coins being struck late in 1849.

All but two coins were melted. One was sent to Secretary of Treasury W.M. Meredith and another to the Mint Cabinet in Philadelphia. The Meredith coin may have gone to the Steven Nagy collection in Philadelphia, but it is unknown to numismatists today. The Mint Cabinet example has been on display in the Smithsonian Institution and is one of the most popular attractions of the numismatic collection. It is reported that J.P. Morgan offered $35,000 for the coin in 1909, a tremendous amount for the era. A gold-plated brass example was offered for sale in the 1892 Woodside Collection but is untraced today. It is possible that someday one of these coins could surface. By any standard, the 1849 Double Eagle is one of the most desirable United States coins ever struck.

It is interesting to ponder what an 1849 Double Eagle could bring on today's market. Although the only known example resides in the Smithsonian Institution, the missing Nagy coin could appear one day. Most experts agree that the 1849 Double Eagle is at least as desirable as the 1933 Double Eagle, if not more so. The pair makes incredible bookends to an extremely popular series and denomination. It can only be speculated what an example would bring if offered for sale. The numismatic community would surely be disappointed if the coin did not set a new price record for a United States coin.

For now, we can all be proud that the only known example of this great coin is on view in the National Numismatic Collection. The coin shares the same showcase with TWO 1933 Double Eagles and an MCMVII (1907) Ultra High Relief Double Eagle. Anyone who has at least a partial interest in coin collecting should make a visit to the Money and Medals exhibit that is part of the Smithsonian Institution. The history of United States coinage is well represented and explained. The Lilly collection of United States and world gold coins that is on permanent display is one of the finest ever assembled of those specialties. Even long-time collectors find themselves in awe whenever they have the opportunity to view the Smithsonian's collection.

Designed by James B. Longacre. The obverse features a portrait of Liberty facing left, wearing a coronet, and surrounded by 13 stars. The reverse features an outspread eagle and shield design. Standards: weight 33.436 grams; composition .900 gold/.100 copper; diameter 34 mm; net weight .96750 ounces pure gold. Edge: reeded.

Rarity: Only one example is known to exist. That specimen now resides in the National Numismatic Collection at the Smithsonian Institution.

Historical Value [estimated, as none have ever come to market]		
Choice Proof		
1960: $100,000	1980: $1,000,000	2003: $7,500,000

1849 DOUBLE EAGLE

Photography courtesy Smithsonian Institution and Douglas Mudd

President Theodore Roosevelt was a great admirer of the famous sculptor Augustus Saint-Gaudens. The two corresponded occasionally after meeting in 1901 at the Pan-American Exposition. First stating his views in 1904, Roosevelt believed that the coinage in circulation at the time was very unattractive and without artistic merit. He wanted coins created that would reflect his affection for the beauty and relief of the ancient Greek coinage. He became excited about the possibility of changing the designs on all U.S. coins. Naturally, he turned to Augustus Saint-Gaudens, who was commissioned to redesign all denominations from the Cent to the Double Eagle.

It was Saint-Gaudens' personal preference that an Indian Head obverse design be used for the Double Eagle. One of the greatest Patterns of this series bears that design. The President was quite insistent, however, that the standing figure of Liberty with the flying eagle reverse be used. Saint-Gaudens used the goddess he had created for the 1903 *Sherman Victory* monument as the motif—Miss Liberty faces forward, holding a palm branch in one hand. In emulation of Greek coins, the design was rendered in very high relief, giving an almost sculpted appearance. As a classic touch, the 1907 date was expressed in Roman numerals, as MCMVII. The Indian Head design was not discarded, but instead was used for the $10 Gold Eagle.

The MCMVII (1907) Ultra-High Relief Double Eagle is an experimental issue. After Augustus Saint-Gaudens became ill, his assistant, Henry Hering, executed the plaster model for his design of the new Standing Liberty Double Eagle. After seeing the proposed design, Charles Barber, the Chief Engraver of the Mint at the time, strongly argued that it would be impractical to strike such a coin since each one required multiple blows from the coining press. Hering knew the relief was too high, but wanted examples struck to test the design. In February of 1907, Hering visited the Mint to check on the striking of the new coin. Hering stated: "...a circular disc of gold was placed in the die and by hydraulic pressure of 172 tons; I think it was, we had our first stamping, and the impression showed a little more than half of the modeling. I had them make a cast of this for my guidance. The coin was again placed in the die for another striking and again it showed a little more of the modeling, and so it went, on and on, until the ninth strike, when the coin showed up in every detail." The resulting treasure from this experiment in striking is one the most coveted coins in numismatics.

The MCMVII (1907) Ultra-High Relief or Extremely-High Relief Double Eagle is a magnificent example of the minting craft. It takes America's most beautiful coin to a new level. Many coins are desirable for their great rarity, but the MCMVII (1907) Ultra-High Relief commands a small fortune because it is literally a work of art. Perhaps no other United States coin, or world coin for that matter, has the visual appeal of the Ultra High Relief. It is truly sad that this gorgeous coin is so expensive and can only be possessed by a very few lucky collectors.

Designed by Augustus Saint-Gaudens. The obverse depicts a standing Liberty draped in Romanesque clothing holding a torch. The reverse features an eagle in the flying position. Mintage for this issue is estimated at 22. Standards: weight 33.436 grams; composition .900 gold/.100 copper; diameter 34 mm; net weight .96750 ounces pure gold. Edge: lettered E PLURIBUS UNUM with words divided by stars. One example is known with a plain edge.

Rarity: There are thought to be 16 to 18 examples known.

Historical Value
Gem Proof
1960: $20,000 • 1980: $250,000 • 2003: $1,000,000

1907 "ULTRA HIGH RELIEF" DOUBLE EAGLE

Photography courtesy Numismatic Guaranty Corporation

The 1894-S Dime is one of the most famous American rarities. While several coins are more rare or more valuable than the 1894-S Dime, few come with the wonderful stories and intrigue that surround this coin.

Depending on which version of which story you hear, the general consensus is that 24 1894-S Dimes were struck. Early explanations of the mintage figure claimed that the 24 coins were made to round out an accounting entry. However, the figure needed was $.40, not $2.40, and the fact that most surviving 1894-S Dimes are Proofs or Proof-like tends to refute that theory; such special coins would never have been necessary to accomplish such a mundane task.

Later research revealed that the Mint Superintendent at San Francisco in 1894, John Daggett, had the coins struck at the special request of banker friends. Of the 24 coins, three went to his young daughter, Hallie, whom he instructed to preserve them carefully until she was older, at which time the coins would be worth a lot of money. Being a typical child, Hallie immediately used one of the 1894-S Dimes to purchase ice cream (thankfully, the coin was later recovered from circulation). However, Hallie clung to the other two, and seventy years later, in 1954, she sold her remaining pair to a California dealer.

No other Barber coin (Dime, Quarter, or Half Dollar) comes even remotely close to the rarity of the 1894-S Dime. Of the original 24 1894-S Dimes, only nine have been positively traced. Two were pulled from circulation (one of them now known appropriately as the "Ice Cream Specimen") while the others are Proof coins in varying degrees of preservation, ranging from impaired to Gem. This raises the tantalizing question, "Where are the remaining 1894-S Dimes?" One would think that with all the publicity surrounding this coin, not to mention the ever-increasing value of this rarity, that other examples would surface. However, such has not been the case, which leads us to question whether the mintage figure of 24 pieces is really accurate. The "real" mintage may be more on the order of 10 or 15 pieces, making the 1894-S Dime approximately twice as rare as is currently believed and putting it on par with the 1804 Silver Dollar (the #1 coin on the Top Ten list and one of the most valuable of all U.S. coins). Perhaps it is time to look at the 1894-S Dime in a new light.

For decades, the 1894-S Dime has been included along with the 1913 Liberty Head Nickel and the 1804 Silver Dollar in a triumvirate of America's most desirable coins. The 1894-S Dime was one of the first coins to cross the $100,000 price barrier and, today, the finest examples are approaching the $1,000,000 mark.

John Daggett was right: the 1894-S Dime has become a very valuable coin!

Designed by Charles Barber. The obverse shows a head of Liberty wearing a freedman's cap, a wreath of laurel tied behind her head, and a band with the word LIBERTY inscribed. The date appears below the head and the words UNITED STATES OF AMERICA form the outer legend. The reverse shows a wreath of American grains and produce surrounding the words ONE DIME. The mint mark appears below the wreath. Standards: weight 38 grains; composition .900 silver/.100 copper; diameter 18 mm; Edge: reeded.

Rarity: 24 struck! Of the nine known examples, two are Gem Proofs.

Historical Value		
Choice Proof		
1960: $15,000 •	1980: $100,000 •	2003: $750,000

1894-S BARBER DIME

1907 INDIAN HEAD DOUBLE EAGLE PATTERN
JUDD 1776

The 1907 Indian Head Double Eagle is a Pattern or experimental issue (Judd 1776 refers to the listing number in the Pattern book written by Dr. J. Hewitt Judd and Abe Kosoff). It is one of the America's most stunning and desirable coins. President Theodore Roosevelt was personally involved in creating this fascinating issue. Roosevelt believed that the nation's coinage was unattractive and without artistic merit. Years earlier, while vice-president, Roosevelt became acquainted with the famous sculptor Augustus Saint-Gaudens, whose works include *Diana*, sculpted in 1892 for the original Madison Square Garden, the *Sherman Victory* monument in New York City, *Hiawatha* for Saratoga New York, and many others. It is not certain when Roosevelt first decided to commission Saint-Gaudens to create a new coinage, but by December 27, 1904, he wrote to Secretary of the Treasury Leslie Mortier Shaw: "I think our coinage is artistically of atrocious hideousness. Would it be possible, without asking permission of Congress, to employ a man like Saint-Gaudens to give us a coinage that would have some beauty?"

The president was also enamored with the beauty and high relief of ancient Greek coinage. At one time, Roosevelt wanted to change the designs of the entire U.S. coinage. Because of the difficulty adapting modern minting techniques to the high relief effects that Roosevelt desired, Saint-Gaudens concentrated his efforts on the Ten Dollar and Twenty Dollar issues.

By means of extensive personal correspondence with the artist at his studio in Cornish, New Hampshire, Roosevelt contributed greatly to the design of this and several issues of the period. He wanted to include the use of an American Indian in full headdress. Saint-Gaudens wrote to Roosevelt in 1907: "…I like so much the head with the head-dress, and by the way, I am very glad you suggested doing the head in that manner." Although Saint-Gaudens preferred the Indian design for the Double Eagle, the Liberty Walking theme was chosen for that denomination. The Indian Head design is similar to the design adopted on the regular issue Ten Dollar coin. In his last letter to the President, Saint-Gaudens wrote: "The majority of the people that I show the work to evidently prefer with you the figure of Liberty to the head of Liberty and that I shall not consider any further on the Twenty Dollar gold coin." At the request of the artist, however, one example was struck for comparison.

The pedigree of this extraordinary coin began with Charles Barber, the Chief Engraver of the U.S. Mint. Waldo Newcomer purchased the coin directly from his estate. The coin was then sold to the prominent collector, F.C.C. Boyd. Boyd's wife sold the coin for a reported $1500 to Abe Kosoff and Abner Kreisberg around 1945. The coin was then sold to King Farouk of Egypt for slightly less than $10,000. After King Farouk was overthrown, his collection of rare coins was auctioned in 1954. The coin sold for approximately $3,444, again to Abe Kosoff, who placed the coin with Roy E. ("Ted") Naftzger, Jr. Dr. J.E. Wilkison obtained the coin in 1956 for $10,000. It was sold in 1973 to Paramount International Coin Corporation as part of the Wilkison Pattern collection. The Wilkison collection was then traded to A-Mark Financial. Judd-1776 was then sold by private treaty to Maryland dealer Julian Leidman in 1979 for $500,000. Jack Hancock and Bob Harwell purchased the coin in the 1981 A.N.A. auction sale for $475,000. Several years later, it was sold to a major northeastern collector of Saint-Gaudens' coinage and is today the cornerstone of that collection.

Designed by Augustus Saint-Gaudens. The obverse features Liberty's head facing left wearing a feathered Indian headdress surrounded by 13 stars. Below the bust, in large letters, is the word LIBERTY. The reverse features a Flying Eagle above a rising sun with the date in Roman numerals. Mintage is reportedly one example. Standards: weight 516 grains; composition .900 gold/.100 copper; diameter 34 mm. Edge: lettered E PLURIBUS UNUM with words divided by stars.

Rarity: Only one example was struck. The coin is a Gem and currently resides in a prominent east coast collection.

Historical Value
Gem Proof
1960: $25,000 • **1980:** $500,000 • **2003:** $7,500,000

1907 INDIAN HEAD DOUBLE EAGLE PATTERN JUDD 1776

Photography courtesy David Akers

One of the greatest numismatic rarities of the twentieth century is the 1943 Bronze Cent. The popularity of this rarity is reflected in its high ranking and the numerous votes it received as a Top Ten coin.

The 1943 Bronze Cents were actually mistakes that caused the government considerable embarrassment. In 1943, the U.S. Mint began using steel blanks (known as "planchets") for the Cents to conserve copper for use in World War II. Over a billion "Steelies" (as they are known popularly) were struck by the three Mints in 1943. The Philadelphia Mint alone produced over 684,000,000 examples. However, a handful of rare 1943 Cents were discovered struck by mistake on old-style, bronze blanks. Presumably, the error occurred when left-over bronze planchets were mixed with a batch of the new steel planchets, and went through the usual striking methods, then escaped into circulation, evading the quality control procedures at the Mint.

Until the 1960s, the Mint's official policy was that it did not make mistakes, despite that its own Chief Engraver once owned a 1943 Bronze Cent. Later, that policy was relaxed, and the Mint now acknowledges the possibility that some 1943 Bronze Cents could have been produced in error.

Rumors of the 1943 Bronze Cent's existence began almost immediately after the coins were struck, but the first real one was not discovered until 1947, when a fellow named Sam Lutes found one in his change. Subsequent discoveries were rare indeed and today, over 50 years later, only a dozen or so Bronze 1943 Cents are known, yielding a discovery rate of one coin every four years. No doubt, this rate will diminish in the future and the 1943 Bronze Cent will remain one of the great rarities of the twentieth century.

Many coin dealers used the 1943 Bronze Cent as a publicity stunt by offering huge rewards for a genuine example (their money was safe because there was little chance that they would ever have to honor their offer). In fact, many of today's collectors started as a result of searching for a 1943 Bronze Cent in pocket change. Another result, a negative one, of the publicity is that coin dealers around the country have had to answer innumerable questions about 1943 Cents, mostly from collectors who are convinced that they have genuine 1943 Bronze Cents. Unfortunately, many of 1943 "Steelies" have been copper-plated and offered as genuine Bronze Cents. As an aid to novice collectors, here's a simple test to determine if your 1943 "Bronze" Cent is really Bronze: if your coin is attracted to a magnet, it's a copper-plated "Steelie"; if not, have your coin checked out by an expert – it may be a new discovery!

Designed by Victor David Brenner. The obverse depicts a bust of Abraham Lincoln facing right, IN GOD WE TRUST above, LIBERTY to the left, and the date to the right. The reverse is plain and understated (but impressive), with ears of wheat on either side, a big ONE CENT in the middle. A smaller E PLURIBUS UNUM appears above and UNITED STATES OF AMERICA appears below CENT. Standards: weight 3.11 grams; composition .950 copper/.050 tin and zinc; diameter 19 mm. Edge: plain.

Rarity: Extremely Rare. Approximately a dozen 1943 Bronze Cents are known. All known examples but one were pulled from circulation, although at least two of those have been certified at the Mint State level. Certain of the finer examples have recently broken the $100,000 barrier.

Historical Value
Extremely Fine
1960: $5,000 • 1980: $20,000 • 2003: $50,000

1943 BRONZE CENT

Photography courtesy Numismatic Guaranty Corporation

The 1822 Half Eagle is certainly one of the most rare, most famous, and most desirable of all United States coins. A scant three specimens are known, although two of these coins are permanently housed in the Smithsonian Institution and will never be owned privately again. Thus, the 1822 Half Eagle is unique in private hands, even though in 1822, the U.S. Mint at Philadelphia produced nearly 18,000 Half Eagles. Other dates of the same period have comparable mintages (some even lower), yet none can compare with the rarity of the 1822.

The extreme rarity of the 1822 Half Eagle stems from the ever-changing relationship of the price of gold relative to that of silver. In 1792, the year the first U.S. Mint was established, the price of gold was approximately 15 times that of silver. At that ratio, a $5 gold piece was worth five Silver Dollars. By the 1820s, the price of silver had dropped due primarily to over-production in Mexican and South American mines making gold worth 18 times that of silver. At that ratio, a $5 gold piece became worth $6, or 20% more than its face value. As a result, virtually all of the earlier American gold coins were pulled from circulation and melted down.

Walter Breen referenced a public assay in Paris in 1831, in which 40,000 U.S. Half Eagles of "recent mintage" were destroyed. Even if this were the only such melting (and it was not), the number of coins destroyed was over twice the entire mintage of the 1822 Half Eagle! Thus, it is easy to see why the 1822 is such a great rarity today. Only a few examples escaped into circulation before the entire remainder of the mintage was destroyed. Many of the early Half Eagles suffered similar fates, but none came close to the near-extinction of the 1822.

For decades, the 1822 Half Eagle was the Holy Grail of United States gold coins. Lorin G. Parmelee, a fabulously wealthy Boston resident, spent years searching for an example in the late 1800s. He finally acquired a piece—only to discover that the coin was counterfeit! When Harlan P. Smith cataloged the Parmelee Collection for auction, the fake was recognized. As coincidence would have it, Smith, himself a major collector of gold coins, had a genuine specimen, which he placed into the sale for "show," but did not allow it to sell. The renowned New York banker J.P. Morgan desperately wanted to own an 1822 Half Eagle, although his numerous attempts were unsuccessful. In 1908, he was outbid at auction for an 1822 Half Eagle, an experience that ultimately haunted him for years. In 1941, Morgan offered a shocking $35,000 to William F. Dunham for his 1822 Half Eagle—a price that was beyond comparison at the time—but once again, he was fruitless in his pursuit. The next time an 1822 Half Eagle was offered for sale (in 1982 as part of the Louis E. Eliasberg Collection), a winning bid of $687,500 was required to buy it. The only coin in private hands now resides in a specialized set of early American coinage, where it surely stands as the collection's cornerstone.

Designed by John Reich. The obverse depicts a large portrait of Liberty, surrounded by 13 stars with the date below. The reverse features an eagle with spread wings, holding an olive branch and arrows. Surrounding the eagle are the inscriptions UNITED STATES OF AMERICA and 5 D., with the motto E PLURIBUS UNUM above the eagle's head. Standards: weight 8.75 grams; composition .9167 gold/.0833 silver; diameter 25 mm. Edge: reeded.

Rarity: Of the three known coins, two are in the Smithsonian.

Historical Value
Extremely Fine
1960: $25,000 • 1980: $650,000 • 2003: $2,500,000

1822 HALF EAGLE

Photography courtesy Tom Mulvaney

Trade Dollars were an interesting run of Silver Dollars spanning the gap between the Seated Liberty design, which ended in 1873, and the Morgan Dollar design, which began in 1878. However, the Trade Dollars were not made for American consumption; they were made specifically for trade in the Orient. In fact, Trade Dollars were legal tender in America only for a short period and, even then, only in amounts up to $5! After their legal tender status was revoked, they traded at a discount in America even though they were heavier than the earlier-minted Seated Liberty Dollars and the soon-to-follow Morgan Dollar.

With the introduction of the Morgan Dollar in 1878, Congress discontinued the Trade Dollar, for political reasons, although it had been a stellar success for its intended purpose—to facilitate commerce with China. From 1879, Trade Dollars continued to be minted in limited quantities for numismatic purposes. The general thought was that 1883 was the last year of the Trade Dollar Proofs. However, from 1907 to 1908, a small number of Proof 1884 and 1885 Trade Dollars came on the market, essentially shocking the numismatic world because none of either date had previously been brought to the notice of collectors.

The source of both the 1884 and 1885 Trade Dollars was William Idler, a coin dealer directly involved with numerous American rarities of dubious origin, including the 1836 "Second Restrike" Half Cent, the Proof Restrikes of the 1801, 1802, and 1803 Silver Dollars, the Class III 1804 Silver Dollar, and others. Idler has been accused of being a fence for Mint employees who needed an outlet for their creations. Even his son-in-law, Captain John Haseltine (also a prominent coin dealer), admitted that Idler was very secretive about his coin collection for fear that some of his coins were subject to seizure. Only five 1885 Trade Dollars are known, a number that has not changed since their first appearance in 1908. Because no records exist of their having been made in 1885 and because of the unusual way in which they entered the market, most numismatic experts believe that they were clandestine pieces made in the Mint. However, this has never diminished their desirability, their rarity, or their value. In fact, the mystery surrounding them has made them even more attractive.

All of the 1885 Trade Dollars were issued only as Proofs, a practice begun with the 1879 Philadelphia Mint Trade Dollars. Unlike the 1884 Trade Dollars (a few of which are also known in copper), no non-silver 1885 Trade Dollars are known. Four of the 1885 Trade Dollars remain in relatively undisturbed condition; the fifth, called "badly cleaned" in the past, was still worth $110,000 in 1980! Today, the 1885 Trade Dollar is one of the few U.S. coins to have broken the $1 million barrier.

Despite their cloudy beginnings, the 1885 Trade Dollars are now readily accepted by the numismatic community, as evidenced by their inclusion in the pantheon of American numismatics: the Top Ten list.

Designed by William Barber. The obverse shows Liberty in a flowing gown facing left and sitting on a bale of cotton and American produce. Her right arm is extended and holds an olive branch. In her left hand, she holds a banner with the word LIBERTY. A small scroll below the bale (and just above the date) bears the motto IN GOD WE TRUST. 13 stars surround Miss Liberty. The reverse shows a plain eagle with outstretched wings, an olive branch in its left talon, and a bunch of arrows in its right. The words UNITED STATES OF AMERICA and a scroll bearing the motto E PLURIBUS UNUM appear above the eagle. The weight and fineness ("420 GRAINS. 900 FINE) and the denomination (TRADE DOLLAR) appear beneath the eagle. Standards: weight 420 grains; composition .900 silver/.100 copper; diameter 38 mm. Edge: reeded.

Rarity: Extremely Rare. Only five examples were struck, all in Proof condition.

Historical Value
Choice Proof
1960: $15,000 • 1980: $100,000 • 2003: $1,000,000

1885 TRADE DOLLAR

The set of 1872 "Amazonian" Pattern coins in gold is one of the most celebrated rarities in the entire series of U.S. coins. This spectacular set is unique many ways: 1) it is the only set ever made, 2) it is the only set of gold Patterns ever produced with a common design theme, and 3) the Three Dollar gold piece in the set is the only Pattern of this denomination ever to have been struck in gold!

In 1872, William Barber produced a relatively large number of Pattern coins, including so-called "Commercial Dollars" (pre-cursors of the 1873 Trade Dollars), "Amazonian" Quarters, Half Dollars, and Dollars with a partially nude Seated Liberty, and "Amazonian" gold coin Patterns that showed just the head of Liberty.

The Amazonian Gold Coin set included Patterns for a Gold Dollar, a Quarter Eagle, a Three Dollar Gold Piece, a Half Eagle, an Eagle, and a Double Eagle. Two sets were struck on aluminum and one set was struck on gold.

The first mention of this spectacular set came in 1886, when R. Coulton Davis included it in a list of known Pattern coins. Later, the set came into the possession of William Woodin, later a Secretary of the Treasury and co-author of the Adams-Woodin Pattern reference book. Subsequently, the set was dispersed, with the Gold Dollar going one way and the other five coins becoming part of King Farouk's collection. When the Farouk collection sold at auction in 1954, Dr. John Wilkison purchased all of the Amazonian gold Pattern coins (there offered as single lots), paying the equivalent of $2,583 for the Double Eagle alone, the highest price of any coin in the sale. Eight years later, in 1962, Wilkison purchased the Gold Dollar, finally reuniting all of the coins in this unique set.

Dr. Wilkison was the foremost collector of gold Pattern coins. Of all the coins in his remarkable collection, Wilkison considered the Amazonian set to be, by far, his favorite.

In 1973, Paramount International Coin Corporation purchased Dr. Wilkison's complete collection of gold Patterns. Dave Akers produced a special, hard cover reference book, highlighting each of the Patterns in the Wilkison collection. At the 1983 American Numismatic Association Convention, the set sold for $418,000 at auction, this at a time when 1913 Nickels were worth around $150,000. Eventually, the set ended up in the collection of gold Proof connoisseur Ed Trompeter, where he, too, considered the Amazonian set to be the crown jewel of his collection. Today, the Gold Amazonian Proof set is believed to be intact in a private collection.

Designed by William Barber. The obverse of each coin features a head of Liberty wearing a freedman's cap bound by a band with the word "LIBERTY" written upon it. 13 stars surround the head; the date "1872" is below the bust. This head is an enlarged version of that used on Barber's Amazonian Pattern Quarters, Half Dollars, and Silver Dollars, thus the appellation was applied to the gold Patterns, as well. The reverse of each coin features an eagle protecting a shield and a scroll that reads "IN GOD WE TRUST." This design is identical on all of the 1872 Silver and Gold Amazonian Pattern Coins.

Rarity: Unique.

Photography courtesy David Akers & Tom Mulvaney

Historical Value
Choice Proof
1960: $15,000 • 1980: $500,000 • 2003: $3,000,000

1909-S VDB LINCOLN CENT

The 1909-S V.D.B. cent has long been considered one of the key dates in the series, filling the dreams of collectors young and old. While the mintage of 484,000 may seem high compared to many other American rarities, one must understand that there are millions of people who collect Lincoln Head Cents. There are simply not enough 1909-S VDB Cents to satisfy all of the collector demand, making this coin a perennial favorite and earning it a place on our list of America's 100 Greatest Coins. Of the Top 100 coins listed thus far, this is the first that is generally available today on a widespread basis.

In 1905, President Theodore Roosevelt commissioned the famous American sculptor and artist Augustus Saint-Gaudens to prepare designs for all denominations including a new Small Cent. Initially, Saint-Gaudens' design for the obverse featured a Flying Eagle motif similar to James Barton Longacre's designs on the Small Cents of 1856-1858. However, this design was abandoned in favor of a head of Victory in profile wearing an Indian headdress. Saint-Gaudens and Roosevelt liked this design so much that they used it for the 1907 $10 gold piece instead of the Cent. Unfortunately, Saint-Gaudens died of cancer before making any more progress on the Cent design, so it was not until 1909 that Victor David Brenner created the famous bust of Abraham Lincoln with which we are all so familiar today.

Brenner's design broke new ground by placing the image of an actual person on a coin made for circulation. In what some naive observers considered to be a break with numismatic tradition, Brenner placed his initials near the bottom of the back of the coin. Despite their small size, the letters V.D.B. were obvious enough that they created an uproar with the public and Mint officials, who immediately demanded their removal. The offending V.D.B. initials were expunged later in 1909, resulting in the creation of four 1909 Lincoln cent varieties for collectors to acquire: 1909 (with and without V.D.B.) and 1909-S (with and without V.D.B.). Of the four varieties, the 1909-S V.D.B. is by far the rarest.

Designed by Victor David Brenner. The obverse depicts a bust of Abraham Lincoln facing right, IN GOD WE TRUST above, LIBERTY to the left, and the date to the right. The reverse is plain and understated (but impressive), with stylized ears of wheat on either side, a big ONE CENT in the middle. A smaller E PLURIBUS UNUM appears above and UNITED STATES OF AMERICA appears below CENT. Standards: weight 3.11 grams; composition .950 copper/.050 tin and zinc; diameter 19 mm. Edge: plain.

Rarity: Scarce. Although the mintage of 484,000 is high compared to the other rarities in this book, the surviving 1909-S VDB Cents are all well distributed among collectors and sometimes require a bit of a hunt to find nice examples.

Photography courtesy Tom Mulvaney

Historical Value
Choice Uncirculated

1960: $150	•	1980: $750	•	2003: $1,500

The 1793 "Chain" Cent, so named because of the connected links that appear on the back, is one of the simplest yet most popular and enduring designs on any American coin.

Despite the promise expressed in the 1792 Pattern coins, the 1793 Chain Cents seem dull and flat, more the work of an inexperienced engraver. The simple design provoked immediate criticism, not only for the quality of the engraving but also for the symbolism expressed on the coin.

Credit for the design goes to Henry Voigt, then Chief Coiner of the Mint, who was also responsible for the 1792 Silver-Center Cents. Voigt must have been terribly embarrassed when the first reviews of his 1793 Chain Cents appeared in several newspapers around the country. Derided for her frightened look, Voigt's Miss Liberty did, indeed, show a woman with flowing, unkempt hair and eyes that conveyed fear, not peace or strength. Furthermore, the back of the coin included a chain of 15 links in a never-ending circle, perceived by the public as representing the bondage and tyranny of the British masters from whom the colonies had so recently freed themselves! Others viewed the chains as representing slavery, a practice common in some parts of the new American nation and reviled in others.

Apart from the aesthetic aspects of the design, the 1793 Chain Cent failed on other counts. The relief detail was so shallow that the design faded after just a short amount of time in circulation. The lack of a highly raised border meant that the design elements had insufficient protection from wear and that the coins would not stack properly. These considerations led to a design change in mid-1793 to the Wreath design (which suffered the same fate as the Chain Cent when it was replaced with the Liberty Cap design even later in the year).

The inexperience of the engraver can be seen on the back of some of the 1793 Chain Cents – some varieties have AMERICA abbreviated as AMERI. because the engraver failed to leave enough room on the coin to spell the word out completely!

Designs attributed to Henry Voigt. The obverse shows a head of Miss Liberty facing right, LIBERTY above, and the date below. The reverse features a chain of 15 links encircling the words ONE CENT and the fraction 1/100. The legend UNITED STATES OF AMERICA appears in a circle near the edge (sometimes with AMERICA abbreviated as mentioned above). Standards: weight 208 grains; composition pure copper; diameter 26 mm. Edge: ornamented with bars and vines.

Rarity: Very Scarce. Over 36,000 Chain Cents were produced, but many have been lost or destroyed over the years. Most survivors are in low grade, but a few exist in magnificent Uncirculated condition.

1793 "CHAIN" CENT

Photography courtesy The Stellar Collection & Tom Mulvaney

Historical Value		
Extremely Fine		
1960: $750	• 1980: $10,000 •	2003: $25,000

The Twenty Cent Piece is one of those well-intentioned coins for which the Mint will be perpetually embarrassed. The new denomination was intended to halt chronic short-changing in the Western States, but was more likely an appeasement to Western silver miners who lost much of their business when the Mint eliminated some of the silver coins in the Mint Act of 1873. The Twenty Cent Piece was basically dead on arrival. Critics derided the confusing similarity between the new coin and the Quarter Dollar. In a classic "history is destined to repeat itself" moment, the Mint made a similar mistake in 1979 by introducing the ill-fated Susan B. Anthony Dollar (also confused with the Quarter Dollar). As a result, the Twenty Cent Piece was made for circulation only in 1875 and the beginning of 1876; Proofs were made from 1875 to 1878.

Although the series was short-lived, from it sprang one of America's most famous rarities, the 1876-CC Twenty Cent Piece.

Early in 1876, approximately 10,000 1876-CC Twenty Cent Pieces were struck and placed in the Mint's vault awaiting release into circulation. In the meantime, Mint officials in the East realized their mistake in creating the new denomination and ordered the destruction of all of the existing stocks of Twenty Cent Pieces, including the 10,000 (or so) 1876-CC's. The melted silver was later turned into other coins and it's interesting to consider that coins exist that were made from a reconstituted 1876-CC Twenty Cent Piece.

Somehow, a few 1876-CC Twenty Cent Pieces escaped the melting pot. Some may have been saved from the annual package of assay coins, originally destined for metallurgical testing back in Philadelphia. However, the number of survivors is greater than the number of coins normally set aside for the Assay Commission, indicating that Mint employees pulled additional examples from the melt itself.

Today, the roster of survivors includes anywhere from 12 to 20 coins, depending on who performs the survey. Most of the known examples are in Uncirculated condition, although at least one example is circulated (could this piece have been pulled from circulation by some lucky collector or was it carried as a pocket piece?).

All 1876-CC Twenty Cent Pieces show doubling of the word LIBERTY on the scroll across the shield on the coin's obverse. This makes it easy to detect 1876 Philadelphia coins with added mint marks, none of which show similar doubling.

Designed by William Barber. The obverse shows Miss Liberty in a flowing gown sitting on a rock. Her left hand holds a staff surmounted by a Liberty Cap; her right hand steadies a shield and holds a band bearing the word LIBERTY. The date appears below the rock and 13 stars surround Miss Liberty. The reverse shows a plain eagle with outstretched wings perched on an olive branch and holding a bunch of three arrows. The outer legends read UNITED STATES OF AMERICA (above) and TWENTY CENTS (below). Standards: weight 77 grains; composition .900 silver/.100 copper; diameter 22 mm. Edge: plain.

Rarity: Approximately 10,000 struck, virtually all of which were destroyed. Almost all of the known examples are Uncirculated, the finest surviving in full Gem condition.

Photography courtesy Numismatic Guaranty Corporation

Historical Value		
Choice Uncirculated		
1960: $7,500	1980: $50,000	2003: $100,000

1907 "ULTRA HIGH RELIEF" DOUBLE EAGLE DIAMETER OF A TEN DOLLAR GOLD PIECE

Most coin collectors are unaware of this incredible issue. The only two surviving examples are housed in the Smithsonian Institution and are seldom displayed. 1907 saw a great deal of experimentation at the U.S. Mint. As mentioned, President Roosevelt was insistent that his friend the sculptor Augustus Saint-Gaudens, redesign the U.S. coinage.

One of the experimental issues produced was a Double Eagle of the MCMVII (1907) design struck on a normal weight planchet, but with the diameter of a Ten Dollar coin. The resulting coin was much thicker than normal. The "Ultra High Relief" Double Eagle was almost double the thickness of a standard Double Eagle (please note the picture of the obverses below) and was smaller than the regular "High Relief" Double Eagle. Moreover, each coin required nine strikings of a 172-ton hydraulic press.

In addition to the excessive strikings, there was also a legal issue. It was and is illegal to mint coins of two denominations using the same diameter planchets. Mint authorities were well aware of this problem. The coin may have been made purely as a novelty. In a letter to the Mint Director (Frank A. Leach) dated January 8, 1908, the Mint Collection curator, T.L. Comparette, stated: "…it is an entirely illegal 'coin' and for that reason should not I believe be put into a collection of historical coins, yet it was produced by the government and for that reason the few specimens will in years after command enormous prices, easily $3000 each. Dealers are now offering large prices for them…" Whatever the motive for the production, the 1907 Ultra-High Relief Double Eagle struck on a Ten Dollar diameter planchet is a captivating piece of minting history and one of America's most alluring coins.

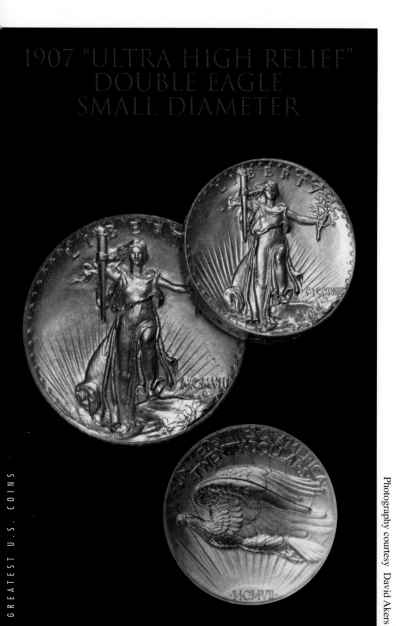

1907 "ULTRA HIGH RELIEF" DOUBLE EAGLE SMALL DIAMETER

Photography courtesy David Akers

Designed by Augustus Saint-Gaudens. The obverse depicts a standing Liberty draped in Romanesque clothing holding a torch, the design taken from the *Sherman Victory* monument. The reverse features an eagle in the flying position. Mintage is reportedly 13 examples. Standards: weight 516 grains; composition .900 gold/.100 copper; diameter 27 mm. Edge: lettering E PLURIBUS UNUM with words divided by stars.

Rarity: Only two examples are known to survive, both in the Smithsonian Institution. A rumor persists of a third example said to have sold early in the twentieth century, but it is currently unaccounted for.

Historical Value
Gem Proof
1960: $20,000 • 1980: $250,000 • 2003: $2,500,000

In 1792, as part of an attempt to develop a national coinage, Mint employees struck approximately 1,500 silver Half Dismes in the cellar of a saw-maker named John Harper. These tiny silver coins bore the image of Miss Liberty on one side and a flying eagle on the other. They were valued at five cents each (or half of a Dime).

Collectors sometimes have trouble pronouncing the word Disme. Is it the phonetically obvious "diz-mee" or is it the traditional way in which we pronounce Dime today (the word into which Disme transmogrified)? Actually, the answer is neither. Disme is a French word pronounced "Deem." Thus, Half Disme is properly pronounced "Half Deem."

A couple of interesting stories surround the 1792 Half Disme. One story suggests that President George Washington provided his own personal silver service to be turned into Half Dismes, yielding enough to distribute to friends, family, government officials, and VIPs. Another is that the likeness on the coin is that of Washington's wife, Martha, who actually bears a strong resemblance to the lady on the coin. Is the 1792 Half Disme a Pattern or a circulation strike?

Generally, Pattern coins are struck in extremely limited quantities (usually fewer than a dozen pieces) just to test how a design will appear in coin form. A mintage of 1,500 pieces suggests that the 1792 Half Disme was much more than just a Pattern, but because they were struck outside the U.S. Mint, because no other Half Dimes were made until 1794, and because the 1792 Half Dismes were not monetized through official channels (as were "real" coins later on), most numismatists consider them to be Patterns. Some experts consider them quasi-official coins, and a smaller group considers them to be one of the first "real" coins made by our U.S. government. Perhaps the best test is that these did indeed circulate as coins, and in December 1792, in his message to Congress, President Washington specifically stated that they had been made as regular coinage. Thus, it is only logical that most known pieces show signs of extensive wear.

Another way to approach the question is to point out the existence of a unique 1792 Half Disme struck in pure copper. Such a piece indicates that the dies were first tested on a blank of base metal, the designs and striking qualities were approved, and a production run of 1,500 Half Dismes began. If the copper piece were the Pattern (or a Die Trial), how can the silver versions that followed be anything other than "real" coins?

Designed by an unknown artist, possibly Birch. The obverse shows a bust of Miss Liberty facing left, her curly hair falling loosely behind her. The date 1792 appears beneath the bust and the legend LIB PAR OF SCIENCE & INDUSTRY (for LIBERTY, PARENT OF SCIENCE & INDUSTRY) encircling. The reverse features a somewhat scrawny eagle in flight with HALF DISME and a star below. The outer legend reads: UNI STATES OF AMERICA. Standards: weight 1.35 grains; composition .8924 silver/.1076 copper; diameter 17.5 mm. Edge: diagonally reeded.

Rarity: Of all the 1792 federal coins, the 1792 Half Disme is the most available today. However, "available" is a relative term when compared with unique and semi-unique pieces so, by any other standards, the 1792 Half Disme is a rare animal, indeed.

1792 HALF DISME

Photography courtesy David Akers & Tom Mulvaney

Historical Value		
Very Fine		
1960: $500	1980: $5,000	2003: $35,000

1838-O HALF DOLLAR

The 1838-O Half Dollar is one of the classic American numismatic rarities, with a reported mintage of a mere 20 pieces. We italicized "reported" because no 1838-O Half Dollars appeared in the annual Director's Report, but the Chief Coiner later stated that 20 examples had been struck and, of course, we have the coins themselves to prove that they had, indeed, been struck.

Why were no 1838-O Half Dollars reported by the Director? The answer may lie in the special circumstances surrounding their production.

Prior to 1838, America's only Mint was located in Philadelphia, Pennsylvania. With the discovery of gold in Georgia and North Carolina in the 1830s, Treasury officials decided to open branch facilities at Dahlonega, Georgia and Charlotte, North Carolina. New Orleans, Louisiana was chosen for a third branch mint, and all three of the new facilities began production of coins in 1838. Dahlonega and Charlotte focused solely on the production of gold coins, while the New Orleans Mint was responsible for both silver and gold coins.

Because many of the known examples appear to have a special finish, experts believe that all of the 1838-O Half Dollars began life as Proof coins. This explains why they were not listed on the Director's report for the year; Proof coins were made in a process separate and apart from the coins made for regular circulation, and they were not included in the totals of the coins handed over to the Treasurer.

The 1838-O Half Dollar was the first Half Dollar produced at a branch Mint and one of the first American coins to bear a mint mark. The placement of the mint mark on the front of the coin was short-lived. In 1840, the mint mark migrated to the back of the coin, where it stayed until 1916.

Although circulation strike examples of the 1839-O Half Dollar were produced, a very small number of this issue also exists in the Proof format. These Proofs have the same surfaces and striking quality as the 1838-O Half Dollar. The 1839-O is actually the rarer of the two issues, but is not as popular because of the circulation strike coins also made for the year.

Designed by Christian Gobrecht (actually a remodeling of John Reich's design). The obverse features a bust of Liberty wearing a freedman's cap with the word LIBERTY on the band. 13 stars circle the bust; the date appears on the bottom of the obverse. The reverse features an eagle, with open wings and a shield on its chest, holding an olive branch and a bundle of arrows. A scroll with the words E PLURIBUS UNUM hovers above the eagle. UNITED STATES OF AMERICA appears near the rims; the denomination 50 C sits beneath the eagle. Standards: weight 206 grains; composition .900 silver/.100 copper; diameter 30 mm. Edge: reeded.

Rarity: approximately one dozen known. Today, the finest 1838-O Half Dollars are two Proof-64 examples, one from the celebrated Norweb collection, the other from the Eliasberg collection (the only complete collection of United States coins ever formed).

Photography courtesy Stack's

Historical Value		
Proof		
1960: $5,000 •	1980: $75,000 •	2003: $200,000

The 1794 Silver Dollar was the first coin of this denomination ever issued by the United States. Ever since numismatics became popular, beginning in the 1850s, the 1794 Silver Dollar has been recognized as a great rarity. One collector, Jack Collins, spent over 30 years tracking all of the known examples, uncovering only 100 demonstrably different examples. In the past few years, a handful of new examples have come to light, bringing the total of known examples to somewhere between 125-150.

The story of the Silver Dollar began around 1792, when the American government deliberated its first coinage system. After careful consideration, the Silver Dollar and the Gold $10 Eagle were made the pillars of the new system, with all other denominations being either fractions or multiples of these two.

Unfortunately, large amounts of silver were simply not available at the time, and the Mint had no funds with which to purchase any. Instead, the Mint relied on depositors who were willing to bring raw silver or foreign silver coins to the Mint for conversion into American silver coins. This meant that each batch of silver had to be processed individually, sometimes more than once. From melting, to refining, to rolling out the ingots into sheets of silver, to punching out the blanks, to the actual coining, each batch was kept separate from all others. Eventually, the depositor would receive a parcel of U.S. coins in an amount equal to the value of the silver that he or she contributed.

Of the 2,000 1794 Silver Dollars coined on October 15, 1794, 242 were rejected as being too poorly struck and having insufficient details. In 1794, the largest coin press at the Mint was the one used to make Cents and Half Dollars. This proved to be inadequate for striking coins as large as the Silver Dollar. In fact, virtually all of the 1,758 coins that survived the quality inspection are still surprisingly weak, a combination of the press capability and the fact that the faces of the dies were not parallel. Thus, finding a well-struck 1794 Silver Dollar is extremely difficult.

Apparently, some of the rejected 1794 Silver Dollars were used as blanks for later Silver Dollars because at least two 1795 Silver Dollars show the undertype of a 1794 Silver Dollar!

Designed by Robert Scot. The obverse shows a head of Miss Liberty facing right, the word LIBERTY above, the date below, eight stars on the left side, and seven stars on the right. The reverse features a plain eagle with outstretched wings within a wreath of palm and olive branches. The outer legend reads UNITED STATES OF AMERICA. No denomination appears anywhere on the coin. Standards: weight 416 grains; composition .900 silver/.100 copper; diameter 39-40 mm. Edge: lettered HUNDRED CENTS ONE DOLLAR OR UNIT.

Rarity: Very Rare. Only 1,758 1794 Silver Dollars were struck, of which an estimated 130 examples survive. One of the finest examples known is the Gem Uncirculated example illustrated to the right.

1794 SILVER DOLLAR

Photography courtesy The Stellar Collection & Tom Mulvaney

Historical Value		
Extremely Fine		
1960: $6,500	1980: $25,000	2003: $125,000

Numismatic treasures await us in the most unlikely places. Take the 1870-S Half Dime, for example. According to official Mint records, none were ever struck, even though six pairs of Half Dime dies were on hand at the San Francisco Mint. Yet, in early 1978, a single example of this previously unrecorded date was purchased as a common type coin. The exciting news of the discovery of an 1870-S Half Dime stunned the numismatic world and, following its exhibition at the 1978 convention of the American Numismatic Association, this previously unappreciated coin sold for $425,000 to Michigan dealer John Abbott. How was the selling price for this unique rarity determined? By a formula agreed to in advance by all parties in which $25,000 was added to the hammer price of the 1804 Silver Dollar sold as part of the John Work Garrett collection!

Accounts of the discovery of the 1870-S Half Dime vary. One account claims the coin was found in a "junk tray," another says a "junk box" (same thing, actually), and a third says it was bought over the counter as a common type coin by a Cook County (IL) dealer.

The cornerstone of the second San Francisco Mint may contain another example of the 1870-S Half Dime along with an 1870-S Three Dollar Gold piece (believed to have been placed there), and possibly other 1870-S dated coins of different denominations.

Coinage from the San Francisco Mint in 1870 varies greatly from modestly scarce to unique. The Double Eagles were the most plentiful with 982,000 coins struck. Today, they are plentiful in circulated condition. Like the 1870-S Half Dime, no Mint records survive for the 1870-S Silver Dollar, though there are currently 12 known examples of the 1870-S Silver Dollar. Both the 1870-S Half and 1870-S Three Dollar are unique. Many of the other issues from this year are quite scarce and seldom encountered.

Although the 1870-S Half Dime is a true giant of numismatics, the coin's value is diminished for a couple of reasons. First, the coin was only recently discovered and has not received the publicity that many of the Top 100 coins have. The coin's size is also a major issue. Half Dimes are very tiny coins. The author recalls an amusing story about this coin from the mid-1980s. A prominent dealer wanted to offer the coin to a client. The owner went to great expense and trouble to have the coin delivered to a convention for his consideration. When presented the coin, the dealer merely said, "It's so small," and handed it back. If the coin were a Silver Dollar, it would probably be one of the most desirable United States coins.

Designed by Christian Gobrecht (obverse) and James Barton Longacre (reverse). The obverse shows Miss Liberty in a flowing gown sitting on a rock. Her left hand holds a staff surmounted by a Liberty Cap; her right hand steadies a shield and holds a band bearing the word LIBERTY. The legend UNITED STATES OF AMERICA appears near the outer rims and the date appears at the base of the obverse. The reverse shows the words HALF DIME within a wreath. The mint mark appears below the word DIME. Standards: weight 19 grams; composition .900 silver/ .100 other; diameter 15.9 mm. Edge: reeded.

Rarity: The only known example has been graded MS-63 by the Professional Coin Grading Service.

Historical Value		
Choice Uncirculated		
1960: $-0-	1980: $425,000	2003: $750,000

The earliest collectors of United States coins formed their collections with virtually no regard to mint marks. It was not until after Augustus G. Heaton's *Treatise on the Coinage of the United States Branch Mints* was published in 1893 that collecting branch mint coinage became popular. The famous Texas dealer B. Max Mehl once stated that when he began his career he paid little attention to where a coin was struck. When numismatists finally began to pay attention to branch mint coins, it became apparent that many issues were very rare. The 1854-S Half Eagle is a star among the many scarce coins that were identified. Only 268 examples were struck for the year. Today, just three coins survive. The reason for the low mintage is still a mystery. It has been speculated that a lack of acid needed to part or refine gold was in short supply and that this may have resulted in the low mintage of Quarter Eagles and Half Eagles. However, a more probable reason is that depositors preferred larger denomination coins as they were easier to store and count. At the time, coins were struck specifically to the order of holders of bullion. Double Eagles, Eagles, and Gold Dollars were made in large quantities in 1854, so the "lack of acid" theory can be dismissed, although the idea was unchallenged until recent times. Whatever the reason, today the 1854-S Half Eagle is a great rarity.

The first auction appearance of an 1854-S Half Eagle was in F.C.C. Boyd collection. The The Numismatic Gallery (Abe Kosoff and Abner Kreisberg) sold Boyd's collection in 1945 and 1946. The 1854-S Half Eagle was sold for the then astounding sum of $5,250 to Louis Eliasberg. The coin remained in his collection until it was sold in 1982. It now resides in a prominent collection. The Boyd 1854-S Half Eagle was graded Extremely Fine in 1946, but by today's standard would be called Uncirculated by most dealers and considered the finest of the three survivors.

1854-S HALF EAGLE

Another example of the 1854-S Half Eagle was obtained privately by B. Max Mehl, who later sold the coin to Col. E.H.R. Green, one of the greatest collectors of his time. Later, the coin changed hands several times and finally became part of the Samuel W. Wolfson collection. Stack's sold the Wolfson collection in 1962 where it realized $16,500. Today, a private collector owns the coin.

The third example of this incredible rarity surfaced in 1919 and became part of the Waldo Newcomer collection. When the Newcomer estate was distributed in the 1930s, B. Max Mehl again sold a specimen to the insatiable Col. E.H.R. Green, who at one time owned two examples. The coin was later part of the Josiah K. Lilly collection, which was donated to the Smithsonian Institution and is now part of the National Numismatic Collection.

Designed by Christian Gobrecht. The obverse portrays Liberty with a coronet facing left and surrounded by 13 stars. The reverse features an eagle with spread wings clutching arrows and olive branches. Mintage is 268 coins. Standards: weight 8.359 grams; composition .900 gold/ .100 copper; diameter 21.6 mm; net weight .24287 oz pure gold. Edge: reeded.

Rarity: The 1854-S Half Eagle may not be the most famous rarity in the United States gold series, but it certainly is one of the most elusive. Only three examples are known, two of which are in private hands.

Photography courtesy Tom Mulvaney

Historical Value
About Uncirculated
1960: $5,000 • 1980: $200,000 • 2003: $750,000

Prior to 1857, One Cent pieces were large pieces of pure copper almost the size of today's Half Dollar. Because of rising copper prices and the ever-increasing costs of production, the U.S. Mint began in 1850 to search for a cheaper and smaller alternative. Finally in 1856, the Mint chose an alloy mixture of copper and nickel that gave the finished product a whitish color, completely unlike any other coins then in production. For the diameter of the coin, government officials settled on a size that has remained ever since, one identical to that of the Cent in your pocket. To differentiate the new coins from the previous "Large" Cents, these smaller coins became known as "Small" Cents.

Technically, the 1856 Flying Eagle Cent is a Pattern meant to illustrate how the design would look as a coin. However, an estimated 2,000-3,000 examples were produced, which is an enormous number by Pattern standards. Presumably, this large number of Patterns was made to spread the word about the significant change that was soon to take place. To make the transition even smoother, the Mint produced both Large Cents and Small Cents in 1857.

The new coins were an immediate success, allowing the Mint to discontinue the production of Large Cents in 1857 and to begin enjoying some cost savings. Unfortunately, the beautiful design was short-lived, ending just two years later in 1858.

There are several different die-varieties known of the 1856 Flying Eagle Cent. The 1856 Flying Eagle Cent is also known in Proof and non-Proof. It is very difficult to determine the striking status for this issue. Many examples are struck with polished dies but are poorly made. When purchasing a coin that is offered as a circulation strike, it is best to consult with an expert.

Designed by James Barton Longacre. The obverse shows an eagle flying left through a plain field. UNITED STATES OF AMERICA appears in an arc above the eagle and the date appears below. The reverse shows the words ONE CENT within a wreath made of ears of corn and other grains. Standards: weight 72 grains; composition .880 copper/.120 nickel; diameter 19 mm. Edge: plain.

Rarity: Rare. Probably 1,500 or so exist today. The Beck Estate hoard had 731 pieces and was dispersed in the 1970s by Abner Kreisberg and Jerry Cohen, remarkably without even a wiggle in the market price, so strong was the demand for such pieces. The 1856 Flying Eagle Cent is available in both Uncirculated and Proof formats. They are usually found in nice condition, as most were recognized as curiosities or rarities when they first appeared.

Photography courtesy Jeff Garrett & Tom Mulvaney

Historical Value		
Choice Proof		
1960: $1,250	1980: $3,500	2003: $15,000

Only one 1873-CC "No Arrows" Seated Liberty Dime is known to exist. Although Mint records indicate a mintage of 12,400 pieces, all were presumed melted in mid-1873 and were most likely turned into Dimes with arrowheads on either side of the date (indicating a slight change in the weight of the coins). The sole survivor is a coin sent to Philadelphia in 1873 to be evaluated by the annual Assay Commission. For some unexplained reason, the coin was saved from destruction and added to the National Numismatic Collection (then known as the Mint Cabinet). Once there, it disappeared from memory until it resurfaced in 1909 as part of the biggest coin trade ever to take place!

In 1909, future Secretary of the Treasury, William Woodin, purchased a pair of gold $50 Patterns (also Top 100 Coins) from dealers Stephen Nagy and John Haseltine. The transaction created a furor at the Mint, which claimed that the unique Patterns were their property. To reverse the transaction, the Mint swapped crates of rare coins and Patterns for the two $50 gold pieces. Included in the trade was the unique 1873-CC "No Arrows" Dime.

Louis Eliasberg purchased the 1873-CC "No Arrows" Dime on November 7, 1950 (it was the last coin he needed to complete his collection of United States coins). Forty-six years later, the silver coins from Eliasberg's collection were sold, and his 1873-CC "No Arrows" Dime fetched $550,000. Since then, the coin has reappeared twice and is now being offered by private treaty for one million dollars. The 1873-CC "No Arrows" Dime is one of only four Carson City Mint coins to appear in the Top 100. The others are the 1876-CC Twenty Cent Piece, the 1873-CC "No Arrows" Quarter Dollar, and the 1870-CC Double Eagle, all of which are extremely rare (but none is unique like the 1873-CC "No Arrows" Dime).

Today, the importance of the 1873-CC "No Arrows" Seated Dime is quite apparent, but that has not always been the case. It must be remembered that early collectors of United States coinage paid very little attention to mint marks. It was not until the 1950s that the true rarity of this great coin was really known.

Designed by Christian Gobrecht (obverse) and James Barton Longacre (reverse). The obverse shows Miss Liberty in a flowing gown sitting on a rock. Her left hand holds a staff surmounted by a Liberty Cap; her right hand steadies a shield and holds a band bearing the word LIBERTY. The legend UNITED STATES OF AMERICA appears near the outer rims, and the date appears at the base of the obverse. The reverse shows the words ONE DIME within a wreath. The mint mark appears below the wreath. Standards: weight 38 grains; composition .900 silver/.100 copper; diameter 18 mm. Edge: reeded.

Rarity: Unique! The only known example is graded Gem Uncirculated (MS-65).

1873-CC "NO ARROWS" DIME

Photography courtesy Numismatic Guaranty Corporation

Historical Value		
Choice Uncirculated		
1960: $25,000	1980: $250,000	2003: $750,000

The MCMVII (1907) High Relief Double Eagle is a masterpiece of the United States series. The coin has a distinct, sculpted appearance. Nearly all collectors consider it one of the most beautiful coins ever produced. This coin is the circulation version of the MCMVII (1907) Ultra High Relief. Theodore Roosevelt personally requested Augustus Saint-Gaudens (a prominent American sculptor of the era) to design new Ten Dollar and Twenty Dollar coins. Roosevelt considered the coin designs at the time to be unattractive and without artistic merit. After Saint-Gauden's death in 1907, Mint Engraver Charles E. Barber was ordered to begin striking the "High Relief" Double Eagles. President Roosevelt even exclaimed, "Begin the new issue even if it takes you all day to strike on piece."

Although the high relief design was fabulous from an artistic standpoint, it was impractical for commercial uses. Bankers complained that the coins would not stack properly, and the high relief design required at least three to five blows from the minting press. The Roman numerals were also too confusing for the American public. Later, in 1907, the relief was dramatically lowered and the Roman numerals replaced with Arabic numerals.

There are two distinct varieties of the 1907 High Relief issues: the Wire Rim and Flat Rim. These varieties were not created on purpose, but were the result of different collars used in the minting process. Loose collars resulted in extra metal being forced between the collar and the dies, resulted in a thin wire rim. On some coins, the wire rim is seen on only one side. The Flat Rim coins are considered to be slightly scarcer, but the Wire Rim and Flat Rim varieties are valued equally in today's markets.

1907 "HIGH RELIEF" DOUBLE EAGLE

Designed by Augustus Saint-Gaudens. The obverse depicts a standing Liberty draped in Romanesque clothing holding a torch. The reverse features an eagle in the flying position. Mintage for this issue is 11,500. Standards: weight 33.436 grams; composition .900 gold/.100 copper; diameter 34 mm; net weight .96750 oz. pure gold. Edge: lettered E PLURIBUS UNUM, with the words divided by stars.

Rarity: Perhaps four to five thousand MCMVII (1907) High Relief Double Eagles survive in all grades. Although only 11,500 were struck, many were saved because of the coin's beauty. The majority of examples seen today are in Mint State condition, some of which are Gems. Well-worn pocket pieces are also seen on occasion. Due to the issue's popularity, MCMVII (1907) High Relief Double Eagles are expensive compared to their relative rarity.

Photography courtesy Tom Mulvaney

Historical Value		
Choice Uncirculated		
1960: $500	1980: $7,500	2003: $15,000

1915-S PANAMA-PACIFIC EXPOSITION FIFTY DOLLAR GOLD PIECES OCTAGONAL AND ROUND

The 1915-S Panama-Pacific $50 gold coins were designed to commemorate the opening of the Panama Canal. Weighing in at nearly 2.5 ounces of gold each, these magnificent coins, also known as "slugs," are very popular with collectors. Their size alone is a compelling reason to admire them. The Panama-Pacific "Fifties" are also very scarce. The Round has a surviving mintage of only 483 pieces, the lowest of any commemorative ever produced. Although 1,509 Octagonal and 1,510 Round examples were originally struck, unsold pieces were melted. Octagonal examples have a slightly higher net distribution figure of 645 coins. The Octagonal and Round issues were sold individually during the 1915 Panama-Pacific Exposition for $100 each. According to the Exposition price list, this entitled the buyer to the commemorative Half Dollar, Gold Dollar, and Quarter Eagle at no additional cost. A framed or leather-cased set of all five coins cost $200. A complete double set, including ten coins mounted in a copper frame (to display both the obverse and reverse), could be had for $400. The seller was Farran Zerbe, professional numismatist and entrepreneur, who held the franchise. These fabulous sets have traded hands for hundreds of thousands of dollars. Mint Superintendent T.W.H. Shanahan produced the first specimens of each denomination in a special ceremony. This set was housed in a special gold presentation case made by Shreve and Co.

At one time, a complete set of Panama Pacific coins in the original frame or box was one of the most desirable items in United States numismatics. Boxed sets regularly traded for over $100,000. The small boxes alone were worth over $5,000 each. The copper frames traded in excess of $20,000. The advent of coin certification changed the demand for original boxed sets. Today, most sets have been broken up with the coins individually graded by a major certification service. The original boxes without the coins are occasionally offered at auction and seldom bring more than $2,000.

Designed by Robert Aitken. The obverse features the head of Minerva, the goddess of wisdom, skill, and agriculture. The date 1915 is presented as Roman numerals MCMXV. On the reverse is an owl seated on the branch of a long-leafed pine tree with very large cones. Eight dolphins at the border encircle the reverse of the Octagonal issue. Net distribution figures for the issue are 645 Octagonals and 483 Rounds. Standards: weight 1290 grains; composition .900 gold/.100 copper; diameter 50.80 mm.
Edge: reeded.

Rarity: Survival of the original net mintage is high, perhaps 80-90%. Many specimens of this issue were kept as pocket pieces, and circulated examples are sometimes encountered. Average Uncirculated (MS-62 to MS-63) coins can be purchased for less than $30,000. Gem examples are very rare and trade for nearly $100,000 each.

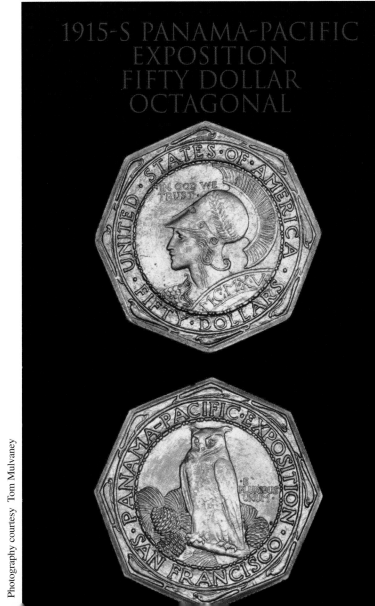

1915-S PANAMA-PACIFIC EXPOSITION FIFTY DOLLAR OCTAGONAL

Photography courtesy Tom Mulvaney

Historical Value (Octagonal)		
Choice Uncirculated		
1960: $2,500 •	1980: $15,000 •	2003: $35,000

Historical Value (Round)		
Choice Uncirculated		
1960: $3,500 •	1980: $20,000 •	2003: $45,000

1875 THREE DOLLAR GOLD

In the field of United States gold coinage, the year 1875 has a magical allure. Indeed, the 1875 Gold Dollar, Quarter Eagle, Three Dollar gold piece, Half Eagle, and Eagle are all formidable rarities. However, the 1875 Three Dollar gold piece has been a long-time favorite among numismatists, given its tiny mintage and perennial fame. In the early 1880s, when it was realized that the $3 denomination might be discontinued (which did happen in 1889), numismatists began to collect the defunct series with vigor. As more and more enthusiasts began to focus on the $3 denomination, the 1875 emerged as a prime rarity.

The 1875 Three Dollar gold piece gained additional notoriety in 1974, when a specimen sold for the then-astounding sum of $150,000. By comparison, an MCMVII (1907) Ultra High Relief—a coin now worth around a million dollars—changed hands in 1974 for $200,000. In fact, the 1875 Three Dollar piece was the first federal gold coin to break the $100,000 mark. However, that high-water mark has never again been met; 1875 "Threes" now sell in the $60,000-$90,000 range.

One possible reason for this decline in value is the specter of restrikes. Although official U.S. Mint records indicate that only 20 specimens were minted of the 1875 Three Dollar gold piece, many numismatic researchers feel that perhaps 30 to 40 were actually struck, of which 20 to 30 may still exist. Thus, the 1875 is actually one of the most common Three Dollar gold pieces in Proof condition! Nevertheless, no circulation strikes were produced and the appeal of the date makes the 1875 Three Dollar gold piece a famous and desirable rarity to this day.

Proof gold coins are considered the ultimate in United States coinage by many. Only the very wealthiest collectors can attempt to complete as series of Proof United States gold coins. One notable collector, who assembled a complete collection, was the late Ed Trompeter. At one time, he owned three 1875 Three Dollar gold coins. Part of his collection was sold at auction in 1992, the remainder sold via private treaty some years later for over 15 million dollars.

Designed by James B. Longacre. The obverse features an Indian princess wearing a feathered headdress. The word LIBERTY is inscribed on the headband. The legend UNITED STATES OF AMERICA is engraved at the perimeter. The reverse depicts the denomination 3 DOLLARS, and the date is encircled by a wreath of corn and grain. Standards: weight 5.15 grams; composition: .900 gold/.100 copper; diameter 20.6 mm. Edge: reeded.

Rarity: 20 to 30 specimens are believed to exist today.

1875 THREE DOLLAR GOLD

Photography courtesy Heritage Numismatic Auctions, Inc.

Historical Value		
Choice Proof		
1960: $7,500 •	1980: $75,000 •	2003: $125,000

1879 AND 1880 FOUR DOLLAR GOLD "STELLAS"

Beginning in the 1870s, several countries advocated the establishment of a universal coin that would correlate to several international currencies. A few efforts were made early in the decade, hence coins such as the 1874 Bickford Pattern Eagles were produced, but the most serious attempts came in 1879. That year, America's minister to Austria, John A. Kasson, proposed a Four Dollar gold coin with a metallic content stated in the metric system, making it easier for Europeans to use. Per Kasson's proposal, this new coin would approximate in value the Spanish 20 Peseta, Dutch 8 Florin, Austrian 8 Florin, Italian 20 Lire, and French 20 Franc piece, among other denominations. The purpose of the $4 gold coin was to facilitate international trade and travel for Americans—the same motivation behind the 1874 Bickford Eagle and other gold Patterns.

Congress became interested enough in Kasson's suggestion to order the Mint to produce a limited run of the Four Dollar gold pieces so that Congressmen could review the coins. Soon thereafter, Chief Engraver Charles E. Barber prepared an obverse design that depicted a portrait of Liberty facing left with long, Flowing Hair. Meanwhile, George Morgan created a motif featuring a portrait with Coiled Hair.

The 1879 Flowing Hair Stella is the most available of the four known varieties, as this was the version produced for Congress. Although 425 pieces were supposedly struck, it is likely that as many as 725 were minted in total. One numismatic legend states that most Congressmen gave their "Stellas" to mistresses as gifts, which would explain the large number of ex-jewelry specimens known today. The other three varieties, the 1879 Coiled Hair, the 1880 Flowing Hair, and the 1880 Coiled Hair are all significantly more rare.

Designed by Charles Barber, the Flowing Hair version features a portrait of Liberty with loose, fluid hair locks. At the edge, the inscription 6 G 3 S 7 C 7 G R A M S is found, indicating the weights and standards of the coin. On the reverse, the eponymous star is located in the center containing the words ONE STELLA 400 CENTS. Circumscribing the star are the words E PLURIBUS UNUM DEO EST GLORIA further encircled by UNITED STATES OF AMERICA FOUR DOL. The Coiled Hair version, designed by George T. Morgan, is similar, with the only difference being the obverse portrait. On the Coiled variety, Liberty is wearing a coronet and the hair is braided. The word LIBERTY is inscribed on the headband. Standards: weight 7 grams (although restrikes vary in exact weight); composition .857 gold/.042 silver/.100 copper; diameter 22 mm. Edge: reeded.

Rarity: 1879 Flowing Hair "Stellas" are by far the most common of the four varieties, with between 300-400 specimens known. The other three varieties are exceedingly scarce and number only a dozen or so survivors.

1879 FOUR DOLLAR GOLD "STELLA"

Historical Value (1879 Flowing Hair)		
Choice Proof		
1960: $5,000 •	1980: $25,000 •	2003: $75,000

Historical Value (1879 Coiled Hair)		
Choice Proof		
1960: $10,000 •	1980: $75,000 •	2003: $250,000

Historical Value (1880 Flowing Hair)		
Choice Proof		
1960: $10,000 •	1980: $ 45,000 •	2003: $125,000

Historical Value (1880 Coiled Hair)		
Choice Proof		
1960: $15,000 •	1980: $100,000 •	2003: $350,000

The 1792 Disme is part of a series of extremely rare Patterns struck at the U.S. Mint, or nearby in private facilities, in anticipation of full production of coins in 1793. Fewer than 20 1792 Dismes are known, most of which are made of copper and only two or three of which are made of silver.

The designs and legends on the 1792 Disme are nearly identical to those on the 1792 Half Disme (also a Top 100 coin). The major difference between the two is the style of Miss Liberty's portrait and the direction in which she faces. Interestingly enough, the head on the 1792 Disme is very similar to that on the 1793 Half Cent, perhaps indicating that the same artist had his hand in all three of the above-mentioned coins. Unfortunately, this design was never used for a Dime. In fact, no Dimes were made until 1796, by which time a new engraver had been hired to create a completely different design. Thus, most collectors have never seen an example of the 1792 Disme other than as a picture in a reference book.

Most known examples have diagonally reeded edges, although at least two examples are known with a plain edge. The purpose of edge reeding was to prevent clipping (shaving or cutting on the edges to remove small amounts of silver which, done enough times on enough coins, could add up to a significant amount of value).

Collecting early United States coinage is once again becoming very popular, as it is now realized that many of these fascinating issues are closely related to the creation of this great nation. In fact, many of our founding fathers were personally involved with the production of these coins. The demand for any early American coin should only increase in years to come.

Designs attributed to a variety of artists, including Adam Eckfeldt and Birch (whose first name has never been verified). The obverse of the coin shows a head of Miss Liberty facing left, her hair flowing wildly behind her. The date appears beneath the bust. The encircling legend reads: LIBERTY PARENT OF SCIENCE & INDUS (the INDUS stands for INDUSTRY). The same legend is found on other 1792 Pattern coins, including the Birch Cent, the Silver-Center Cent, and the Half Disme. The reverse shows the word DISME below an eagle in flight. UNITED STATES OF AMERICA makes up the outer legend. Standards: weight 58-61 grains for the copper versions, slightly less for the silver versions; composition pure copper or silver, respectively; diameter 23 mm. Edge: reeded or plain.

Rarity: Extremely Rare. Fewer than 20 examples are known.

Photography courtesy Larry Hanks

Historical Value
Extremely Fine (Copper)
1960: $1,000 • 1980: $17,500 • 2003: $75,000

Although this book describes many prohibitively rare coins, very few coins can claim the status of being "Unique." Even in the field of American gold coinage—an arena laden with extreme rarities—only a handful of select rarities are truly unique. One of these is the 1870-S Three Dollar gold piece, a coin whose history remains somewhat uncertain, even after extensive research.

In 1870, construction began on a new United States Mint in San Francisco. To commemorate the new facility, the previous San Francisco Mint facility struck specimens of each coinage denomination so that the coins could be placed in the cornerstone. What research has not been able to determine, however, is whether these coins were actually placed inside. What numismatists do know is that two reverse dies were shipped from Philadelphia to San Francisco, neither of which bore the appropriate "S" mint marks. Apparently, an employee hand-engraved the mint mark onto one of the dies, from which either one or two Three Dollar gold pieces were struck.

The only known example of the 1870-S Three Dollar gold piece appears to have been placed in a piece of jewelry, as it exhibits evidence of minor cleaning and has the numerals "893" engraved on the reverse. Despite these flaws, the coin sold for $687,500 in 1982 and is now valued at over $1,000,000. It is now on display at the American Numismatic Association Museum in Colorado Springs, Colorado as part of the Harry W. Bass Reference Collection. Although many Bass coins were sold at auction, the 1870-S Three was retained as the prize of the collection, along with a full collection of other $3 gold dates and mints, an incredible cabinet of gold coins of all denominations from 1795-1834, plus a selection of Patterns and currency.

Now that the 1870-S Three Dollar is permanently housed in a museum, no other complete sets of Three Dollar gold coins may be completed. Several other coins in the United States series are similarly out of reach. The 1849 Double Eagle, housed in the Smithsonian, is another example.

Designed by James B. Longacre. The obverse features an Indian princess wearing a feathered headdress. The word LIBERTY is inscribed on the headband. The legend UNITED STATES OF AMERICA is engraved at the perimeter. The reverse depicts the denomination 3 DOLLARS, and the date is encircled by a wreath of corn and grain. Standards: weight 5.15 grams; composition: .900 gold/.100 copper; diameter 20.6 mm. Edge: reeded.

Rarity: Only one 1870-S Three Dollar gold piece is known, thus determining this incredible rarity's value is difficult. Although the exact amount may be debatable, numismatists would agree that if the Bass coin were ever sold again, the million-dollar mark would surely be exceeded.

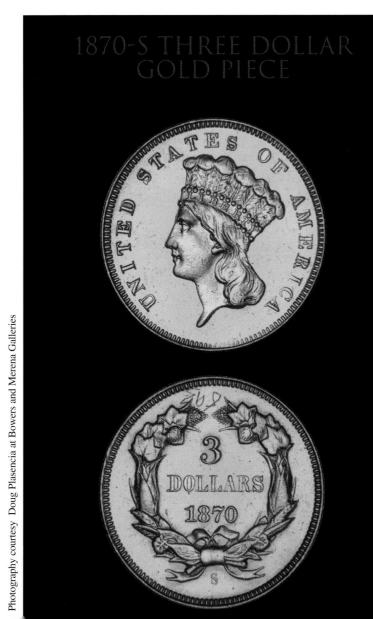

Photography courtesy Doug Plasencia at Bowers and Merena Galleries

Historical Value		
Very Fine		
1960: $25,000	1980: $650,000	2003: $2,500,000

The 1792 Silver-Center Cent is extremely rare and represents the first bi-metallic coin produced by the American government. The 1792 Silver-Center Cent was a Pattern piece, struck to test both the new design and the unusual two-part alloy in anticipation of full production of Cents in 1793.

In 1792, the public's perception of coins was much different from what it is today. Then, if a coin did not contain its full value in metal, merchants refused to accept it in payment or discounted it heavily. This was especially true for gold and silver coins, but copper coins were also subject to the same demands. Unfortunately, one Cent of pure copper in 1792 translated into a very large and heavy coin.

To reduce the size of the Cent, the Mint considered adding a small amount of silver to replace a lot of the copper. In one version, the copper and silver were melted and mixed together, but it was impossible to tell by looking at the coin whether it contained any silver at all. Thus, counterfeiters could have made a lot of money simply by leaving the silver out of the mixture and making their copies out of pure copper.

To solve the problem, the Chief Coiner of the Mint, Henry Voigt, advocated placing a small plug of silver in the middle of a copper coin, bringing the value up to one Cent. A small hole was drilled in the center of a copper blank, a plug of silver was inserted, and the coin was struck, flattening out the silver plug so that it filled the hole completely.

1792 SILVER-CENTER CENT

While the concept was ingenious, the technique was inefficient and unsuitable for mass production. In the end, the Mint officials decided to make the One Cent out of pure copper.

The lore of the 1792 Silver-Center Cent increased with the discovery of some interesting examples. In 1911, while the original U.S. Mint was being demolished, workmen found some old copper planchets (blanks) with holes drilled through the centers. These were the same size as the 1792 Silver-Center Cents and, most likely, the intent was to turn them into coins with the addition of a silver plug. Then, in 1994, a struck Silver-Center Cent was discovered without the silver plug and with no traces of a plug ever having been inserted, although there was a hole in the proper position.

Designs attributed to Henry Voigt. The obverse shows a head of Miss Liberty facing right, her disheveled hair falling loosely behind her. The date appears beneath the bust. The encircling legend reads: LIBERTY PARENT OF SCIENCE & INDUST (the INDUST stands for INDUSTRY). The same legend is found on other 1792 Pattern coins, including the Birch Cent, the Half Disme, and Disme. The reverse shows the words ONE CENT within a wreath. The fraction "1/100" appears beneath the bow of the wreath. UNITED STATES OF AMERICA makes up the outer legend. Standards: weight 72 grains; composition pure copper with a small plug of silver; diameter 23 mm. Edge: reeded.

Rarity: Extremely Rare. Less than a dozen examples are known of the 1792 Silver-Center Cent. The finest examples are two fully Uncirculated pieces, one of which realized $414,000 in early 2002.

Historical Value		
Very Fine		
1960: $1,500 •	1980: $25,000 •	2003: $85,000

The Fugio Cent is the first officially sanctioned United States coin struck in quantities large enough that collectors can afford to collect them. Much of the charm of these coins comes from the interesting design elements, some of which are attributed to the plain-speaking American statesman, Benjamin Franklin. The Fugio Cents are very similar in appearance to the 1776 Continental Dollar (No. 12 in the Top 100).

Following its short-lived coinage of 1776 pewter dollars, the successors to the Continental Congress tried a different approach in 1787. This time, rather than try to create its own Mint, Congress contracted with a private coiner to strike Fugio Cents. The deal was advantageous for both parties; the government would loan the coiner over 71,000 pounds of copper at a good price to get him started, and he would repay the loan with the coins he made. The winner of the contract was required to strike 345 tons of coins and would receive a percentage of anything he coined.

Through bribery and political machinations, James Jarvis (who had no mint, no machinery, and no employees versed in coining) won the contract. Jarvis immediately purchased a controlling interest in the company that also held the contract to produce copper coins for the state of Connecticut. To obtain additional copper to fulfill the contracts, Jarvis left for England. While he was gone, his representatives struck roughly 9,000 pounds of Fugio Cents, but appropriated the rest of the government's copper to make Connecticut Coppers.

When Jarvis failed to obtain the necessary copper, he defaulted on the contract, never paying a cent for the rest of the metal loaned to him by the American government.

According to some historians, Fugio Cents were not received very well at the time they were struck. The public was wary of the new and unusual design, preferring instead the old copper coins then in circulation. However, it is likely that most—but not all—served the intended purpose. Somehow a small hoard of Fugio Cents (reportedly a keg of approximately 5,000 pieces) ended up in the vaults of the Bank of New York. They were released slowly over the years, even as late as the 1950s, although some remain today. A few years ago, the colonial coin expert Tony Terranova examined them and filed a report for interested numismatists. Were it not for this hoard, Uncirculated Fugio Cents would be very rare and expensive.

Today, the Fugio Cent is one of the most popular and desirable of all American coins.

Designed by James Jarvis, copying designs from the 1776 Continental Currency pewter Dollar. The obverse shows a sundial with a sun and rays above. The motto MIND YOUR BUSINESS appears beneath the base of the sundial. FUGIO appears on the left side of the coin; the date 1787 on the right. The reverse shows a never-ending chain of 13 links surrounding a circular label with WE ARE ONE in the center and STATES UNITED surrounding. Standards: weight 150-160 grains; composition pure copper; diameter 28-29 mm. Edge: plain.

Rarity: Common (although some varieties are extremely rare). Many are struck on imperfect planchets.

Historical Value		
Uncirculated		
1960: $50 •	1980: $500 •	2003: $2,500

At one time, this incredibly rare coin was considered a Pattern or experimental issue. It has been shown, however, to be a regular issue United States coin struck for general circulation. In 1860, Anthony Paquet, an engraver at the Philadelphia Mint, modified the reverse design for the Double Eagle. The new design is very similar to the standard issue, but the reverse letters are much taller and slender in appearance. There are also several technical variations with regard to the positioning and size of the lettering. In late 1860, the Paquet reverse became the standard design that was adopted for the regular issue coinage of 1861 Double Eagles. Dies were shipped to the branch Mints of New Orleans and San Francisco. Actual coinage on high-speed presses began in January of 1861 in Philadelphia. It was feared that the wider fields and narrow rim would cause breakage of the dies, so the use of planchet dies was discontinued. However, those dies that were used for coinage experienced no problems at all, proving their withdrawal was unnecessary.

Mint Director James Ross Snowden recalled the new design and ordered the melting of the 1861 Double Eagles made at the Philadelphia Mint. The entire Philadelphia run was destroyed, with the exception of a few coins. Snowden also ordered production to cease in New Orleans and San Francisco. The order reached New Orleans in time to prevent any coinage. Because the transcontinental railroad was still several years from completion, and the telegraph did not extend past St. Joseph, Missouri, word to stop coinage did not reach San Francisco until 19,250 coins had been struck. Charles H. Hempstead, Superintendent of the San Francisco Mint, replied to the instructions on February 9, 1861: "...I was unable to prevent the striking and issuing of a large number of double eagles, coined with the new dies." No effort was made to recall the issue.

Today, just two examples of the Philadelphia mintage are known of this extremely rare coin. Of the 1861-S version made in San Francisco, several hundred exist.

Designed by James B. Longacre. The obverse features a portrait of a Coronet Liberty facing left and is surrounded by 13 stars. The reverse features an outspread eagle and shield design. Mintage for this issue is unknown. Standards: weight 33.436 grams; composition .900 gold/.100 copper; diameter 34 mm; net weight .96750 oz pure gold. Edge: reeded.

Rarity: Only two examples are known from the Philadelphia Mint. One coin, in About Uncirculated condition, was part of the Dallas Bank Collection sold by Sotheby's and Stack's in 2001. That coin was discovered in Paris in the 1970s. The other surviving example is Gem Uncirculated and traces its pedigree to 1865 (when the coin was sold by W. Elliot Woodward for $37). The coin subsequently resided in many famous collections, among them those of Ambassador and Mrs. R. Henry Norweb, King Farouk, and Colonel E.H.R. Green.

1861 "PAQUET REVERSE" DOUBLE EAGLE

Photography courtesy Numismatic Guaranty Corporation

GREATEST U.S. COINS

Historical Value		
About Uncirculated		
1960: $5,000	1980: $75,000	2003: $350,000

By 1792, the United States prepared to open its first official Mint. Land was purchased, buildings were torn down and erected, machinery was ordered, and a variety of artists began preparing dies for coins.

One such artist, with a last name of Birch (we're not really sure of his first name), engraved dies for a large One Cent piece to be made of pure copper. The earliest versions of Birch's Cent, known today by a unique piece in white metal, showed Miss Liberty with a much smaller hairdo of curlier hair. Also, on the original version, the back of the coin bore "G.W. PT." (for George Washington – President) in place of the 1/100 fraction and a smaller ribbon bow. Birch probably changed the design because Washington objected to having his image (or any reference to him) placed on a coin. Birch's final version, as illustrated above, is one of the most popular of all American Pattern coins.

According to Mint records, a small purchase of copper was made on September 11, 1792, enough to make between 100 and 200 Birch Cents. This is consistent with the present rarity of this piece, which now numbers in the vicinity of a mere handful of examples. Versions are known with edges that are plain or lettered with "TO BE ESTEEMED BE USEFUL." The obverse of the Birch Cent bears a strong resemblance to the design on the 1792 Half Disme, suggesting that Birch may have had a hand in that design, as well.

Of the three types of 1792 Pattern Cents (Silver-Center Cent, Fusible Alloy Cent, and the Birch Cent), the Birch Cent matches most closely the standards set forth in the Mint Act of 1792. Thus, a strong argument can be made that this is the first official United States Cent: they were struck at the United States Mint by Mint employees, on Mint equipment, and made according to official government standards well in advance of the Cents of 1793.

Collecting early United States coinage is again very popular, as it is now realized that many of these fascinating issues are closely related to the creation of this great nation. Many of our founding fathers were personally involved with the production of these coins. The demand for any early American coin should only increase in years to come.

Designed by Mr. Birch. The obverse features a bust of Miss Liberty facing right, with her hair flowing behind her. The date 1792 appears below the bust. The encircling legend reads: LIBERTY PARENT OF SCIENCE & INDUSTRY. The reverse features the denomination ONE CENT within a wreath, with the fraction 1/100 just below the ribbon bow. The outer legend reads: UNITED STATES OF AMERICA.

Rarity: Extremely Rare.

Photography courtesy Smithsonian Institution and Douglas Mudd

Historical Value		
Very Fine		
1960: $1,500	1980: $35,000	2003: $200,000

The 1848 discovery of gold in California created special problems for certain of its inhabitants. The massive influx of people, coupled with inflation and a lack of coins with which to conduct business, led to great difficulties. Gold dust became a de facto currency, but measurements varied, often to the detriment of the owner of the dust (the size of a "pinch" of gold was directly related to the size of a man's finger and thumb). Private minters moved in to fill the void, producing a variety of gold coins of somewhat suspect quality and purity.

To help solve the problem, a United States Assay Office was created in 1851 in San Francisco, under the direction of Augustus Humbert. He contracted with the firm of Moffat & Company to produce massive $50 coins (legally termed "ingots") with eight sides and nearly 2.75 troy ounces of pure gold. Known today as "Slugs," these big and heavy coins created a new level of confidence with the general public, essentially driving the underweight and impure coins out of circulation. Unfortunately, the "Slugs" failed to address the need for smaller denomination coins.

Because they were technically ingots and not coins, the $50 Slugs were not required to be of the same 90% purity as federal gold coins. Thus, four different finenesses appear on the $50 Slugs: .880, .884, .887, and .900. The earliest versions had lettered edges; later version had reeded edges. Some varieties required as many as 14 steps to produce a single coin!

Although they were produced in large quantities, most of the $50 Slugs were melted down and converted into United States gold coins once the San Francisco Mint began operations in 1854. Today, $50 Slugs are prized, impressive reminders of an important part of our American heritage.

Although thousands of United States Double Eagles were found in the wreckage of the steamer *SS Central America*, which sank in 1857, very few Fifty Dollar "Slugs" were discovered, most of which were Augustus Humbert issues. When the great treasure was first discovered, it was speculated that "Slugs" would become much more available. The opposite has occurred because the publicity of the *SS Central America* has created increased demand for all territorial gold coins.

Designs by Charles Cushing Wright and Augustus Humbert. The obverse shows an eagle on a rock, clutching a shield, a bundle of arrows, and an olive branch. The eagle holds a scroll in its beak. A scroll above the eagle states the fineness of the coins (.e.g., 800 THOUS.) "UNITED STATES OF AMERICA" and the denomination surround the eagle. The outer margins will be plain or lettered, depending on the variety. The reverse is an engine-turned design, sometimes with a target in the center and sometimes with the number "50" (for the denomination) punched in the center. Standards: weight 83.50 to 85.50 grams, depending on fineness; composition 88 to 90% gold, the remainder silver and trace metals; diameter 41 mm edge to edge. Edge: reeded or lettered, depending on the variety.

Rarity: Very Scarce. Uncirculated examples are very rare. A few Proofs are known, including a piece that brought $500,000 over 20 years ago!

Historical Value		
Extremely Fine		
1960: $1,500	1980: $6,500	2003: $15,000

In the early nineteenth century, large United States gold coins were never in great demand by the general public. Since the average merchant or citizen rarely handled such grand amounts of money, there was rarely a need for large denominations. As official records indicate, there were three gold deposits at the Mint: one on June 24, 1815 from a Mr. Thomas Parker; a second on October 30 from The Bank of Pennsylvania, and a holding of earlier-dated gold still at the Mint. These three deposits were melted together, and portions of it were struck into exactly 635 Half Eagles. Interestingly, there was over $3,600 worth of gold sitting in the Mint ready to be converted into coin the next year, but a fire at the Mint on January 11, 1816 damaged some rolling and cutting equipment, which precluded further production for a time.

Relatively few of the original 635 specimens minted have survived. It is estimated that a dozen coins are currently known, many of which were likely pulled from circulation long ago. Indeed, the average survival rate for an early U.S. gold coin is under 2%, and over half of the existing pieces show no wear or only minimal circulation.

The 1815 Half Eagle is a tried and true classic—and in the nineteenth century, before mint marks were generally collected and before the true rarity of the 1822 Half Eagle was known, the 1815 was the most famous of all American gold coins, with no close competition! This is an interesting illustration of the changing perceptions and popularity trends over the years.

The 1815 Half Eagle has been long considered very rare. In 1859, Dr. Montroville W. Dickeson wrote in his book, *The American Numismatic Manual*, " The Mint Report gives a coinage of 635 pieces for the year. We have never met one of them.." That is quite a statement given that his work was the first substantial study of United States coinage.

Designed by John Reich. The obverse features a large portrait of Liberty surrounded by 13 stars with the date below. The reverse depicts an eagle with spread wings, holding an olive branch and arrows. Surrounding the eagle are the inscriptions UNITED STATES OF AMERICA and 5 D., with the motto E PLURIBUS UNUM above the eagle's head. Standards: weight 8.75 grams; composition .9167 gold/.0833 silver; diameter 25 mm. Edge: reeded.

Rarity: Approximately 12 coins can be pedigreed with certainty, although the possibility remains that an additional coin or two still exists.

1815 HALF EAGLE

Photography courtesy Tom Mulvaney

Historical Value		
Extremely Fine		
1960: $2,500 •	1980: $45,000 •	2003: $100,000

The Strawberry Leaf Cent is an extremely rare variety of the 1793 Wreath Cent type (the one that shows Liberty on the front with Flowing Hair and no cap, and a wreath on the back). Years ago, conventional wisdom was that these were Patterns, never mind that all known pieces are extensively worn (unlikely for a Pattern coin). Either way, the Strawberry Leaf Cents have a rich tradition in American numismatics that goes back many years.

In place of the normal, three-leaved sprig just above the date, the Strawberry Leaf Cent sports a curious cluster that looks, to many people, like a clump of three strawberries. No one knows why the engraver made this change, but the front and back of the Strawberry Leaf Cent are sufficiently different from the normal Wreath Cent to suggest that a different person made each. Others have suggested that they may be contemporary counterfeits. Their extreme rarity, interesting stories, and high degree of popularity make them one of the most sought-after of all American coins. Just mention the words "Strawberry Leaf" to Large Cent collectors and watch their expressions.

A Guide Book of United States Coins attributes the Wreath Cent design to Henry Voigt, while Walter Breen assigns it to Adam Eckfeldt. In spite of some hearsay evidence to the contrary, the authors doubt if either man engraved the dies, since neither had the requisite skill, nor was either man trained as an engraver. However, because the die work on the Strawberry Leaf Cents is somewhat cruder than that on the Wreath Cents and if, indeed, we look at the Strawberry Leaf Cents as Patterns of some sort, then it is distinctly possible that Voigt had a hand in these dies.

1793 "STRAWBERRY LEAF" LARGE CENT

Designed by Voigt, Eckfeldt, or some other artist. The obverse front depicts a head of Liberty facing right, with a sprig of "strawberry" leaves just above the date. Above the head is the word LIBERTY. The reverse features the words ONE CENT surrounded by a wreath within the legend UNITED STATES OF AMERICA. The fraction 1/100 appears beneath the bow of the wreath. Standards: weight 208 grains; composition pure copper; diameter 27 mm. Edge: vine and bars.

Rarity: Only four examples are known. One example has not been seen for many years, but its pedigree is legitimate, and supposedly it rests in a private collection. A second example is unique in that its reverse is different from all the others. A third example is in the American Numismatic Society's collection. The fourth example appeared on the market in 1992 when it was sold (along with the second example just mentioned) as part of R.E. "Ted" Naftzger's fabulous collection of Large Cents; both of these are now "locked away" in a complete collection of Sheldon varieties. Walter Breen reported a fifth example, but the existence of this piece has never been confirmed. The finest specimen known is in only Very Good condition (the missing coin mentioned above). The next best is in Good condition!

Photography courtesy William Noyes & Jon Lusk

Historical Value		
Fine		
1960: $2,500	1980: $30,000	2003: $200,000

1798 "SMALL EAGLE" HALF EAGLE

Although the Mint Act of April 2, 1792, provided for a gold Half Eagle of 135 grains weight and other denominations, no gold coins were produced until 1795. Around May of that year, Philadelphia Mint Director David Rittenhouse assigned engraver Robert Scot the task of producing Half Eagle dies. Rittenhouse left the Mint at the end of June and was replaced by Henry William DeSaussure, who ordered that gold coin production should begin. When the Half Eagle debuted, it featured a design known today (per terms mostly devised by Kenneth E. Bressett for use in *A Guide Book of United States Coins)* as Capped Bust Right, Small Eagle Reverse.

The obverse depicts Miss Liberty facing right wearing a Liberty cap with the word LIBERTY above and the date below. The Small Eagle reverse motif was apparently taken from an ancient Roman onyx cameo that depicted an eagle perched on a palm branch, its wings outstretched, holding aloft a circular wreath in his beak. The inscription UNITED STATES OF AMERICA is featured at the periphery. Strangely, there is no indication of denomination on the piece, but then again, most eighteenth-century merchants weighed all coins and made value decisions based on their own findings.

This design lasted until 1798. The Heraldic Reverse was also struck during this time period. Why so many designs and die combinations were used during such a short time is a mystery. It has been suggested that Mint operations were chaotic in the early years of operation. Regardless of the reason, many great rarities were created. The 1798 Small Eagle Reverse Half Eagle is a classic American rarity.

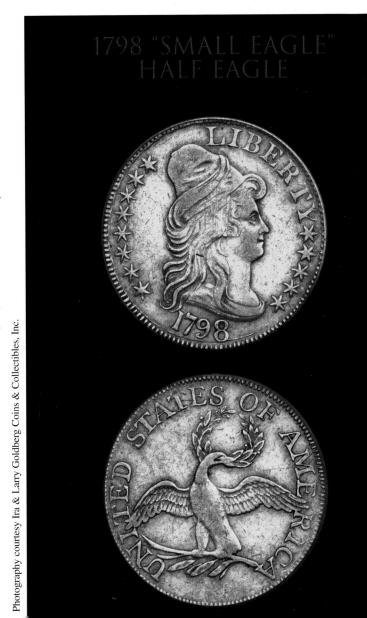

The author handled an example of this great rarity in the mid 1980s. The coin had been advertised in *Coin World* magazine. A gentleman called one day to inquire about the availability of the piece and to get a price quote. After hearing the price, he hung up. A few days later, the mystery man arrived with the asking price in cash. Anonymity was requested, and the coin was sold and has not been seen since.

Designed by Robert Scot. The obverse depicts Liberty wearing a soft liberty cap and facing left. The stars are placed around the obverse rim, and the date is located at the base of the obverse. The Small Eagle reverse shows an outstretched eagle wearing a shield of 13 stripes. The wings are partially covered by a flowing scroll inscribed E PLURIBUS UNUM. Clouds are placed above the eagle's head. Standards: weight 8.75 grams; composition .9167 gold/.0833 copper; diameter 25 mm. Edge: reeded.

Rarity: Of the eight examples known, three are in museums. The most recent discovery surfaced a few years ago and was purchased by John Dannreuther of Tennessee.

Photography courtesy Ira & Larry Goldberg Coins & Collectibles, Inc.

Historical Value
Extremely Fine
1960: $3,500 • 1980: $75,000 • 2003: $250,000

These coins' first public appearance was in the 1890 sale of Lorin G. Parmelee's collection. Both an 1844-O Half Eagle and 1844-O Ten Dollar in Proof (a specially made coin with a mirror finish) were sold at the same sale. In the Parmelee auction, the Ten Dollar was catalogued as "Eagle: O mint sharp and perfect Proof: as it is allowable to strike Proofs only at the Philadelphia Mint, it would seem that this lot and the following (the Proof 1844-O $5 gold half eagle) must be extremely rare." The buyer of both coins was William Woodin at $16 and $9.5, respectively. The coins later appeared in Thomas L. Elder's sale of Woodin's Collection in 1911.

After selling for $50 in 1911, the 1844-O Proof Eagle disappeared from the coin market for the next 84 years (Many believe that a U.S. diplomat held the coin for over 80 years.) The coin finally surfaced in 1994 and created a sensation in the rare coin market. For many years, the rumored existence of the Proof 1844-O Eagle only added to its mystique. The late Texas dealer Mike Brownlee heard about the coin in the 1950s while working for the legendary B. Max Mehl. He searched for the coin his entire numismatic life. His search ended in 1994 when he was finally able to purchase the 1844-O Proof Eagle for an undisclosed amount. The Half Eagle was sold by Abe Kosoff in 1959 and now resides in a private collection.

Why the 1844-O Half Eagle and Eagle were struck in the first place is the real mystery. It is possible the coins were struck for a dignitary of this country or some foreign head of state visiting the New Orleans Mint. Possibly a presentation set of coins was made for the outgoing Southern President John Tyler or for the incoming Southern President James K. Polk. Perhaps someday researchers will solve the puzzle of these two incredible coins.

1844-O
PROOF EAGLE

Designed by Christian Gobrecht. The obverse portrays Liberty with a coronet facing left and surrounded by 13 stars. The reverse features an eagle with spread wings clutching arrows and an olive branch. Mintage is thought to be only one of each coin. Half Eagle Standards: weight 8.359 grams; composition .900 gold/.100 copper; diameter 21.6 mm; net weight .24287 oz pure gold. Edge: reeded. Eagle Standards: weight 16.718 grams; composition .900 gold/.100 copper; diameter 27 mm; net weight .48375 oz pure gold. Edge: reeded.

Rarity: Each coin is Unique; only one Choice Proof example of each is known to exist.

Photography courtesy Robert Lecce

Historical Value (Half Eagle Proof)		
Choice Proof		
1960: $2,500	1980: $75,000	2003: $850,000

Historical Value (Eagle Proof)		
Choice Proof		
1960: $2,500	1980: $75,000	2003: $1,250,000

The 1884 Trade Dollar is shrouded in mystery and intrigue. Unknown until 1907, the 1884 Trade Dollar first appeared when a small hoard of six pieces came on the market, all from the same source. Those six pieces have since been dispersed, along with several other pieces that have appeared on the market. Whenever an 1884 Trade Dollar comes up for sale, it always creates considerable excitement.

Tradition has placed the mintage of the 1884 Trade Dollar at 10 coins (all Proofs), a figure that is actually supported by Mint records. Thus, the 1884 Trade Dollar has a somewhat greater claim to legitimacy than does the 1885 Trade Dollar (another Top 100 coin), for which no Mint records exist. The late Carl W.A. Carlson, a talented researcher who at different times worked for Paramount, NASCA, and Stack's, felt that the 1884 Trade Dollar was a "legitimate" issue, a regular Proof, but that only 10 were made.

A small number of copper 1884 Trade Dollars are known, at least three of which were silver-plated and offered as genuine 1884 silver pieces!

For the last seven years, the 1884 Trade Dollar has appeared at auction at the rate of one coin per year. However, this frequency is elevated because of the sale and resale of one coin that had been off the market for decades. Most of the 1884 Trade Dollars sold in recent years have gone into strong hands, and it is unlikely that they will re-appear anytime soon.

Designed by William Barber. The obverse shows Miss Liberty in a flowing gown facing left and sitting on a bale of cotton and American produce. Her right arm is extended and holds an olive branch. In her left hand, she holds a banner with the word LIBERTY. A small scroll below the bale (and just above the date) bears the motto IN GOD WE TRUST. 13 stars surround Miss Liberty. The reverse shows a plain eagle with outstretched wings, an olive branch in its left talon, and a bunch of arrows in its right. The words UNITED STATES OF AMERICA and a scroll bearing the motto E PLURIBUS UNUM appear above the eagle. The weight and fineness ("420 GRAINS. 900 FINE) and the denomination (TRADE DOLLAR) appear beneath the eagle. Standards: weight 420 grains; composition .900 silver/.100 copper; diameter 38 mm.
Edge: reeded.

Rarity: Extremely Rare. Only 10 examples were struck, all in Proof condition.

Photography courtesy Ira & Larry Goldberg Coins & Collectibles, Inc.

Historical Value		
Choice Proof		
1960: $7,500	1980: $50,000	2003: $200,000

The 1873-CC "No Arrows" Quarter Dollar was supposedly made in a quantity of 4,000 pieces, yet only five examples are known to have survived. Most assuredly, the Quarter Dollar suffered the same fate as the 1873-CC "No Arrows" Dime (now unique), essentially being wiped out in a melt in 1873. At least one of the Quarter Dollars came from the same package of 1873-CC coins sent to the Assay Commission for analysis, plus a few more of the Quarter Dollars must have been spared from destruction by some other means.

In looking at the price trends for major rarities, a reasonable conclusion is that these special coins increase in price over time. However, the air at the top is rarified, and many factors affect the price of blue-chip coins. Factors include economic conditions, market timing, the simultaneous appearance of more than one example of a rarity, auction fever, auction venue, and a buyer or seller's decision to hold the coin for an extended period. When the MS-62 Eliasberg 1873-CC "No Arrows" Quarter Dollar re-entered the market in 1997, it realized $187,000 after spirited bidding. Exactly two years later, the same coin sold for $106,375, a rather substantial loss for the seller, but a relative bargain for the buyer, since the finest known 1873-CC "No Arrows" Quarter Dollar (an MS-64) sold in the meantime for $209,000! Timing is everything. For rarities, including the majority of pieces in the Top 100 coins, handsome price increases have been the rule, and hardly ever the exception, if quality pieces are bought with care and held for the long term. However, in the short term, as illustrated above, profits are sometimes elusive.

Although the 1873-CC "No Arrows" Quarter Dollar is a great rarity, as recently as 1996, a previously unknown example surfaced. The coin had once belonged to an antique dealer from the 1940s and 1950s, and had been handed down without realizing the coin's true rarity.

Designed by Christian Gobrecht (obverse) and James Barton Longacre (reverse). The obverse shows Miss Liberty in a flowing gown sitting on a rock. Her left hand holds a staff surmounted by a Liberty Cap; her right hand steadies a shield and holds a band bearing the word LIBERTY. 13 stars appear in an arc above Miss Liberty, and the date appears below the rock at the base of the obverse. The reverse shows an eagle with a shield on its chest, an olive branch in its right talon, and a bunch of arrows in its left. A scroll with the words E PLURIBUS UNUM hovers above the eagle. The words UNITED STATES OF AMERICA appear above the eagle; the abbreviations QUAR. DOL. appear below. The mint mark appears between the bottom of the eagle and the denomination. Standards: weight 96 grains; composition .900 silver/.100 copper; diameter 24.3 mm. Edge: reeded.

Rarity: Five known. The finest known 1873-CC "No Arrows" Quarter Dollar, an MS-64, sold for $209,000 in 1998.

Historical Value		
Uncirculated		
1960: $3,500	1980: $75,000	2003: $175,000

The 1849-C "Open Wreath" Gold Dollar is the undisputed "King" of the Gold Dollars, if not one of the scarcest United States gold coins. Not only is it an extreme rarity, but also the coin is veiled in mystery. After gold was found in the hills of North Carolina, a Congressional Act was passed in 1835 allowing for the establishment of a mint in Charlotte. Three years later, the Charlotte Mint opened, producing Quarter Eagles and Half Eagles exclusively. In 1849, Congress passed another Act mandating that a One-Dollar coin be struck in gold. The dies for the Gold Dollar were made in Philadelphia and then sent to Charlotte. Two reverse dies were prepared: one with a closed wreath and a second featuring an open wreath. Although both dies were delivered to Charlotte, the majority of the Gold Dollars struck were from the "Closed Wreath" die. Perhaps the "Open Wreath" die was used for a short trial run.

Unlike most of the coins documented in this book, the 1849-C Open Wreath remained unknown to numismatists for decades after it was struck. The first specimen came to light in 1933, when prominent Baltimore collector Waldo Newcomer offered a specimen for sale. After it resided in another collection for about ten years, the coin was acquired by Dallas numismatist Robert Schermerhorn. Soon after he bought the discovery piece, a second specimen surfaced. W.W. McReynolds, a jeweler who lived in Schermerhorn's neighborhood, found the new coin. A few numismatists felt the coincidence was uncanny, suspecting that McReynolds copied Schermerhorn's coin. However, research has proven that the controversial piece is genuine. In all likelihood, McReynolds stumbled upon the coin in a piece of jewelry because it exhibits noticeable mounting marks. Schermerhorn consigned his specimen to the 1956 ANA auction, where it realized a then-remarkable $6,000. Since then, the coin has changed hands many times, selling privately for six figures multiple times. In addition to the two pieces mentioned earlier, a third and forth specimen have come to light. Even with the total population reaching four, this variety still commands incredible sums of money at auction.

Designed by James B. Longacre. The obverse features an emblematic figure of Liberty wearing a coronet. The word LIBERTY is inscribed on the headband. 13 stars are engraved at the periphery. The reverse shows the legend UNITED STATES OF AMERICA engraved at the perimeter. Inside is a wreath, in the center of which is the denomination 1 DOLLAR and the date. Standards: weight 1.672 grams; composition .900 gold/.100 copper; diameter 13 mm. Edge: finely reeded.

Rarity: Exactly four specimens are known. Interestingly, one of these pieces has been described in catalogs all the way from Very Fine to Mint State! It is appropriate to mention here that Gold Dollars have formed a special focus of interest for one of the authors (Garrett), who is now working with John Dannreuther in the gathering of technical data for the entire series 1849 to 1889.

Photography courtesy Doug Winter

Historical Value
Extremely Fine
1960: $7,500 • 1980: $75,000 • 2003: $275,000

Congress originally established a relative value of silver to gold at 15 to 1. This proved inaccurate, as the true marketplace value was closer to 16 to 1. The result was that early United States gold coinage could be melted and sold for more than its face value in terms of silver. That is why so many early issues are rare today. In 1804, the Mint suspended production of the Ten Dollar denomination. The Act of June 28, 1834 reduced the weight of gold coins, thereby eliminating the incentive to melt gold coinage. However, for the time being, only $2.50 and $5 gold coins were minted. In July of 1838, the Secretary of Treasury ordered the resumption of production for the $10 denomination. Christian Gobrecht prepared new dies and coinage began late that year. On December 6, 1838, four specimen "Proofs" were delivered to the Secretary of Treasury. Today, three examples still survive of this incredibly beautiful coin. One piece was placed in the Mint Cabinet and now resides in the Smithsonian Institution and is part of the National Numismatic Collection. A second specimen found its way into the collection of the infamous King of Egypt Farouk and was sold in the 1954 palace sale along with three other coins for only $590. That coin was purchased by John Jay Pittman, who considered it his premier U.S. Proof gold coin. When his collection was sold at auction in 1998, the 1838 Proof Eagle alone realized $550,000. The third example, a Gem Proof, resides in a private collection.

The design for the Ten Dollar gold coins was modified slightly in 1840, thus creating a scarce two-year Type. Proof United States gold coins are considered the ultimate in desirability, both for their beauty and rarity. Early Proof gold coins are extremely rare, especially high denomination coinage. The 1838 Proof Eagle is one of the premier rarities of the United States series.

1838 PROOF TEN DOLLAR GOLD

Although the desirability of this issue cannot be overstated, it is notable that the 1838 Proof Ten Dollar gold is one of the greatest first-year issues created. Early examples of United States coinage in Proof are extremely rare and desirable.

Designed by Christian Gobrecht. The obverse features a portrait of Liberty facing left surrounded by 13 stars. The reverse has an eagle with wings spread clutching arrows and an olive branch. Mintage for this issue is four Proofs. Standards: weight 16.718 grams; composition .900 gold/.100 copper; diameter 27 mm; net weight .48375 oz pure gold. Edge: reeded.

Rarity: Today three Proof examples of this date are known. One is in the Smithsonian and the remaining two are now in private collections.

Photography courtesy David Akers & Tom Mulvaney

Historical Value		
Choice Proof		
1960: $5,000	1980: $100,000	2003: $500,000

In 1804, the production of Ten Dollar gold coins halted. The high intrinsic value of gold made the coins worth more than their face value. Regular production of reduced weight Ten Dollar gold coins did not resume until 1838. In 1834, however, a very interesting issue of coins was specially minted. A November 11, 1834 letter to Samuel Moore, Director of the Mint, from John Forsyth of the State Department explains why these coins were struck: "Sir: The President has directed that a complete set of the coins of the United States be sent to the King of Siam, and another to the Sultan of Muscat. You are requested, therefore, to forward to the Department for that purpose, duplicate specimens of each kind now in use, whether of gold, silver, or copper. . . ." In due course, the instructions were followed, and Proof Sets, each fitted into a special presentation case, were struck for diplomatic purposes for the Far East.

The problem arose that the Silver Dollar and the Ten Dollar gold coins were no longer being struck and therefore were not current. In an effort to include all denominations that had been struck by the United States Mint, it was decided to check production records to determine when the last coins of those denominations were made. Mint records indicated that 19,570 Silver Dollars and 3,757 Ten Dollar coins had been made in 1804. Mint officials in 1834 who created new versions of the coins did not realize that the Silver Dollars had been struck with earlier dated dies, thus they inadvertently created a classic rarity. New dies were made for an 1804 Silver Dollar and Ten Dollar gold piece for inclusion in the 1834 Proof Sets. The newly designed Ten Dollar gold coin differed slightly from the original, the most notable changes being the last digit of the date and the arrangement of the denticles inside the rim. The original 1804 Ten Dollar gold coins were struck with a Crosslet 4, while the 1834 Restrikes, dated 1804, were made with a Plain 4. Moreover, unlike the $10 gold coins originally struck in 1804, the new 1804-dated $10 coins were struck in a Brilliant Proof format, giving them a stunning appearance.

Today, one of the 1834 diplomatic presentation sets still exists, complete except for two coins. Numismatists call this the "King of Siam Set" and consider it to be one of the crown jewels of coin collecting. Three other examples of the 1804 Ten Dollar "Plain 4" variety exist. Several examples of this fascinating rarity are also known in silver, but it is not certain they were made in 1834. Perhaps they were struck at a later date, possibly 1859 (when extensive restriking began) or later. The 1804 Ten Dollar gold piece in Proof is one of the earliest dated examples of Proof gold coinage from the United States and is highly desirable for that reason. The coins are also closely related to the legendary 1804 Silver Dollar, assuring their status as one of the greatest United States coins.

Designed by Robert Scot. The obverse features a capped bust of Liberty facing right surrounded by 13 stars. The reverse displays an heraldic eagle clutching 13 arrows and an olive branch. Mintage for the issue is unknown. Standards: weight 17.50 grams; composition .916 gold/.083 silver and copper; diameter 33 mm. Edge: reeded.

Rarity: Four examples are currently thought to exist. One still resides in the fabulous "King of Siam" set and another is part of the Harry Bass Collection, which is on long-term loan to the museum of the American Numismatic Association in Colorado Springs, Colorado. The remaining two are in private collections.

1804 "PLAIN 4" TEN DOLLAR GOLD

Photography courtesy Numismatic Guaranty Corporation

Historical Value		
Proof		
1960: $3,500	1980: $50,000	2003: $150,000

The 1866 "No Motto" Seated Liberty Quarter Dollar is considered unique. The "Motto" refers to the scroll bearing the words "IN GOD WE TRUST," added to the backs of Quarter Dollars beginning in 1866. Thus, some experts consider the 1866 "No Motto" Quarter Dollar to be a transitional Pattern, a sort of missing link that bridges the old "No Motto" Quarter Dollars and the new "With Motto" Quarter Dollars. Without any other evidence, such a conclusion is perfectly logical and implies exceptional value and desirability. However, the 1866 "No Motto" Quarter Dollar was probably not made in 1866, but years later! Its history is unknown, but this and related "No Motto" high-denomination silver coins were not known to the collecting community until the twentieth century.

According to Walter Breen, the 1866 "No Motto" Quarter Dollar is "...a fantasy piece, struck in a set with the Half Dollar [Judd 538] and Silver Dollar [Judd 540], long after authorization to adopt the new design with motto (Act of March 3, 1865). This set was made up for the Mint's favorite druggist, Robert Coulton Davis. Calling them transitional pieces destroys the meaning of the term; the true transitionals are the 1865 coins with motto as adopted in 1866."

The three coins remained together as they passed through some significant collections, including those of William Woodin (Secretary of the Treasury), Colonel E.H.R. Green (son of Hetty Green, the "Witch of Wall Street"), and King Farouk of Egypt. Eventually, the set became part of the DuPont family's collection. Then, in 1967, five masked gunmen robbed the Willis H. DuPont family in their Florida home and took the set of 1866 "Patterns" and other valuable coins.

1866 "NO MOTTO" QUARTER DOLLAR

Photography courtesy American Numismatic Association

For over 30 years, the whereabouts of many of the stolen DuPont coins remained a mystery. While some coins were recovered over the years, the 1866 "Patterns" remained hidden until late 1999, when a Los Angeles coin company purchased the Quarter Dollar in "a lot of junk and old electrotype Colonial coins." The significance of the coin was soon discovered, the proper owners were notified, and the coin was returned to the DuPont family. They, in turn, loaned the coin to the American Numismatic Association, where the 1866 "No Motto" Quarter Dollar is proudly (and securely) displayed along with the DuPont's 1866 "No Motto" Half Dollar!

The last sale record for an 1866 "No Motto" Quarter Dollar was in 1961, when the DuPont family acquired the coin from the Edwin Hydeman collection for $24,500 (a huge price at the time). Edward Hydeman, from York, Pennsylvania, was a long-time collector who operated Wiest's Department Store in that city. He also had some other Top 100 coins, including an 1804 Dollar and a 1913 Liberty Head Nickel, not to overlook an 1894-S Dime!

Designed by Christian Gobrecht. The obverse shows Miss Liberty in a flowing gown sitting on a rock. Her left hand holds a staff surmounted by a Liberty Cap; her right hand steadies a shield and holds a band bearing the word LIBERTY. 13 stars appear in an arc around Miss Liberty, and the date appears at the base of the obverse, below the rock. The reverse shows an eagle with a shield on its chest, an olive branch in its right talon, and a bunch of arrows in its left. The words UNITED STATES OF AMERICA appear above the eagle; the abbreviations QUAR. DOL. appear below. Standards: weight 16.25 grams; composition .900 silver/.100 copper; diameter 24.3 mm. Edge: reeded.

Rarity: Unique!

Historical Value		
Choice Proof		
1960: $25,000	1980: $75,000	2003: $350,000

The story of the 1866 "No Motto" Seated Liberty Half Dollar is very similar to that of the 1866 "No Motto" Quarter Dollar (another Top 100 coin). Both coins are unique, both were part of the same three-piece set (including the 1866 "No Motto" Quarter Dollar, the 1866 "No Motto" Half Dollar, and the 1866 "No Motto" Silver Dollar), and both were stolen from the DuPont family collection in 1967. From that point, however, their paths separated, only to meet again more than 30 years later, under uncannily similar circumstances and almost at the same time.

The word "Motto" refers to the scroll bearing the words "IN GOD WE TRUST," authorized by a Congressional act in March 1865 but not added to the backs of Half Dollars until 1866. Some experts consider the 1866 "No Motto" Half Dollar to be a transitional Pattern, but others believe they were made years later at the request of a Mint "insider." Some collectors even speculate that a special set of the Quarter Dollar, Half Dollar, and Silver Dollar was made for Robert Coulton Davis, a druggist, turned informant for the Mint, whose help enabled the Mint to recover 1804 Dollars in an 1858 operation. Thus, the words "fantasy coin" and *"pièce de caprice"* can be used to describe this unique rarity, similar to the 1866 "No Motto" Quarter Dollar, which is also now on display at the American Numismatic Association museum in Colorado Springs, Colorado following its recovery.

The last sale record for an 1866 "No Motto" Half Dollar was in 1961, when the DuPont family acquired the coin from the sale of the aforementioned Edwin Hydeman collection for $15,500 (an extremely high price for the time).

Designed by Christian Gobrecht. The obverse shows Miss Liberty in a flowing gown sitting on a rock. Her left hand holds a staff surmounted by a Liberty Cap; her right hand steadies a shield and holds a band bearing the word LIBERTY. 13 stars appear in an arc above Miss Liberty, and the date appears at the base of the obverse, below the rock. The reverse shows an eagle with a shield on its chest, an olive branch in its right talon, and a bunch of arrows in its left. The words UNITED STATES OF AMERICA appear above the eagle; the abbreviation HALF DOL. appears below. Standards: weight 192 grains; composition .900 silver/.100 copper; diameter 30 mm. Edge: reeded.

Rarity: Unique!

Photography courtesy American Numismatic Association

Historical Value
Choice Proof
1960: $20,000 • 1980: $75,000 • 2003: $350,000

1866 "NO MOTTO" SILVER DOLLAR

Only two 1866 "No Motto" Seated Liberty Dollars are known to exist. These special coins are identical to the regular Silver Dollars of 1866 except for one small detail that might easily be overlooked: there is no scroll with "IN GOD WE TRUST" above the eagle on the reverse. The motto was added to the reverse of most U.S. coins in 1866, including the Silver Dollar, following five years of development. This coin completes our trio of "No Motto" 1866 silver coins, except that two specimens are known of the Silver Dollar, whereas only one each is known for the Quarter Dollar and Half Dollar.

The seed for the motto came from an 1861 letter written by the Reverend M.R. Watkinson, of Ridleyville, Pennsylvania, to the Secretary of the Treasury, Salmon P. Chase, in which Watkinson bemoaned the lack of a reference to God on American coins. Chase responded favorably and quickly, and by December 1861, Pattern Half Dollars and Eagles were produced with the experimental motto GOD OUR TRUST. In 1864, the motto IN GOD WE TRUST was adopted and was introduced to the general public on the new Two Cent piece. In 1866, the motto was added to all U.S. Silver coins valued at 25 cents and up, and all U.S. gold coins valued at $5 and up.

Several of the "With Motto" Pattern coins of 1863-1865 have been shown to be from dies used first in 1866 and 1867. The 1866 "No Motto" coins may have been fabricated to create deliberate rarities, a theory contrary to the previously held belief that they were transitional Patterns. Whether they were made as numismatic rarities, or for whatever reason, virtually all "numismatic delicacies" are highly collectible today. While their parentage is very interesting to study, as here, most collectors concentrate on their rarity, fame, and display value!

1866 "NO MOTTO" SILVER DOLLAR

One of the 1866 "No Motto" Silver Dollars was part of a three-piece set (along with the Quarter Dollar and Half Dollar) owned ultimately by the DuPont family and stolen in 1967 in an armed robbery. The 1866 "No Motto" Quarter Dollar and 1866 "No Motto" Half Dollar (both unique and both Top 100 coins) were recovered later, but the 1866 "No Motto" Silver Dollar still remains missing.

A second 1866 "No Motto" Silver Dollar re-surfaced in the 1970s before entering a private midwestern collection in the early 1980s.

Designed by Christian Gobrecht. The obverse shows Miss Liberty in a flowing gown sitting on a rock. Her left hand holds a staff surmounted by a Liberty Cap; her right hand steadies a shield and holds a band bearing the word LIBERTY. 13 stars appear in an arc around Miss Liberty, and the date appears at the base of the obverse, below the rock. The reverse shows an eagle with a shield on its chest, an olive branch in its right talon, and a bunch of arrows in its left. The words UNITED STATES OF AMERICA appear above the eagle; the abbreviation ONE DOL. appears below. Standards: weight 26.7 grams; composition .900 silver/.100 copper; diameter 38 mm. Edge: reeded.

Rarity: Two known. The last public auction of an 1866 "No Motto" Silver Dollar was in 1972!

Photography courtesy Numismatic Guaranty Corporation

Historical Value		
Choice Proof		
1960: $15,000	1980: $100,000	2003: $1,000,000

The 1833 Proof Half Eagle is considered one of the greatest United States coins mainly on the merits of the magnificent specimen from the John Jay Pittman collection, brought to market by David W. Akers. Pittman, an employee of Eastman Kodak in Rochester, New York, collected coins over a long period of time and was able to acquire many rarities that others overlooked. This 1833 Half Eagle is deeply mirrored, well struck, and is in virtually the same state as the day it was made. This wonderful Half Eagle is also richly toned and fully original. It is simply a breathtaking example of early United States gold coinage.

As a date, the 1833 Half Eagle is also very rare. Fewer than 75 circulation strike examples are thought to have survived. Early United States gold coins were worth more for their bullion value than for the coins' face value, so the survival rate for these early issues is minuscule. For the year 1833, there are two varieties: the Large Date and Small Date. There are two Proofs known for the year, both of which are of the Large Date variety. Besides the Pittman coin, there is also an example of this rare issue in the National Numismatic Collection, which is housed in the Smithsonian Institution.

The Pittman coin has a long and illustrious pedigree. It was once a part of the collections of J. Colvin Randall, Lorin G. Parmelee, James Flanagan, Jake Bell, and King Farouk. John Jay Pittman purchased the coin in Egypt in 1954 when the collection of the deposed ruler was sold at public auction. The coin realized 210 Egyptian Pounds, the equivalent at the time of about $600. In 1997, the coin was sold for $467,500 at the Pittman estate auction!

Like the Pittman example of this great coin, the specimen that resides in the National Collection is of Gem quality. It is quite lucky that the coin has remained so nice. For many years, the gold coins are very nice, but the silver coins were harshly cleaned during the last two centuries. Some well-meaning employees of the museum would occasionally clean the tarnished silver coins. Luckily, the gold coins did not tone and were spared the hash treatment.

Designed by William Kneass, a modification of the John Reich design. The obverse features a capped Liberty facing left surrounded by 13 stars. The reverse displays an heraldic eagle clutching arrows and olive branches. Mintage is unknown. Standards: weight 8.75 grams; composition .900 gold/.100 copper; diameter 23.8 mm. Edge: reeded.

Rarity: Two examples are known in Proof. One is in the Smithsonian and the other is part of a private collection.

1833 PROOF HALF EAGLE

Photography courtesy David Akers & Tom Mulvaney

Historical Value
Gem Proof
1960: $3,500 • 1980: $100,000 • 2003: $500,000

In mid-1834, William Kneass extensively redesigned the Half Eagle and Quarter Eagle denominations, creating what is now known as the Classic Head type. On the obverse, Miss Liberty faces left with stars surrounding her head and with the date below. On the reverse, an eagle holds a shield on its breast; it is perched on an olive branch and holds three arrows. The inscription UNITED STATES OF AMERICA, 5 D. can be found near the edges. This type is also known as the "No Motto" version because the words E PLURIBUS UNUM were eliminated. In addition to the obvious stylistic changes, the weight was reduced from 135 grains to 129 grains due to the Act of June 28, 1834. This was a badly needed weight modification, as many early gold coins were melted because their bullion value exceeded their face value. Consequently, Classic Head gold coins are more common than earlier types.

While Classic Head circulation strikes are abundant, the Proof versions are not. At most, twenty Classic Head Half Eagles are known in Proof, and, of these, a few are either damaged or permanently held in museums. The 1834 is the most "common" of the group. One resides in the fabulous King of Siam set. There are several deceptive first strikes, but probably 12-15 true Proofs are known. The 1835 was well represented in the Pittman Collection by two of the three known examples of the date. The third known specimen is a part of the Smithsonian Collection. There are also only three examples known of the 1836 Half Eagle in Proof. Again, the Pittman Collection contained a Gem example, the Smithsonian Collection has one, and the third was contained in an original 1836 Proof set purchased by Brian Hendelson in 1996. 1837 is represented by a unique example in the Smithsonian Collection. Finally, the only known 1838 Proof is reported to be a part of the Byron Reed Collection in Omaha, Nebraska.

1834 PROOF CLASSIC HEAD HALF EAGLE

There are several die varieties of the 1834 Proof Classic Half Eagle. Although this would only be of interest to specialists of United States gold coins, on one variety of the Proof examples for this year, the eagle's tongue is missing.

Designed by William Kneass. The obverse features a head of Liberty facing left surrounded by 13 stars. The reverse displays an heraldic eagle clutching arrows and olive branches. Mintage for these issues is unknown. Standards: weight 8.36 grams; composition .899 gold/.100 silver and copper, changed to .900 gold in 1837; diameter 22.5 mm. Edge: reeded.

Rarity: The Proof coins in this series range from 12-15 known for the 1834, to unique for the 1837 and 1838. Any Proof Classic Head Half Eagle must be considered a major rarity and is usually seen only when great collections are sold.

Photography courtesy David Akers & Tom Mulvaney

Historical Value		
Choice Proof		
1960: $2,500 •	1980: $25,000 •	2003: $65,000

Despite a mintage of 180,000 coins, the 1927-D is one of the rarest dates in the entire Double Eagle series. Though 1927 was too early for the coins to have been affected by the gold recall of 1933, it seems that the entire mintage was destroyed, except for a handful of survivors.

One interesting possibility exists as an alternative to the "melt theory" to explain the rarity of the 1927-D Double Eagles: they may, in fact, still be hidden in some European vault!

Millions of American gold coins were shipped to Europe from around 1879 to 1933, for international payments. Often, foreign banks, merchants, and other interests wanted gold or "hard money," not printed paper bills. After America stopped paying out gold coins in 1933 and later asked for their return from the American public, the foreign banks held on to them more tightly than ever! Following World War II, many long-stored Double Eagles and other coins were found in vaults in Switzerland (in particular), France, Venezuela and elsewhere, much to the delight of numismatists! Later, word spread and a modern gold rush was on! Probably, most rarities have been discovered by now, but who knows? In the case of the 1927-D, fewer coins may have gone to Europe because of the lower initial mintage; in any case, no quantities of this date have yet been discovered in Europe or, if they have, no one is talking.

At one time, the true rarity of the 1927-D Double Eagle went unrecognized. Several other dates were considered much more rare, including the 1924-D and 1926-D, both later found by the hundreds in Europe. However, unlike those other dates, the 1927-D Double Eagle remains a great rarity. As time passes and the European gold stocks dwindle, the likelihood of any 1927-D's showing up becomes smaller and smaller.

Designed by Augustus Saint-Gaudens. The obverse depicts a Standing Liberty draped in Romanesque clothing and holding a torch. The reverse features an eagle in a flying position. Mintage for this issue was 445,500, but nearly all examples were melted. Standards: weight is 33.436 grams; composition .900 gold/.100 copper; diameter is 34 mm; net weight .96750 ounces of pure gold. Edge: lettered includes E PLURIBUS UNUM with the words divided by stars.

Rarity: Extremely Rare. Only a dozen or so examples are known to exist, most of which are in Choice to Gem condition.

1927-D DOUBLE EAGLE

Photography courtesy David Akers & Tom Mulvaney

Historical Value		
Gem Uncirculated		
1960: $1,500 • 1980: $150,000 • 2003: $500,000		

1829 HALF EAGLES
LARGE AND SMALL PLANCHETS

In 1829, Chief Engraver William Kneass modified the obverse motif on the Half Eagle, and the diameter was reduced to 23.8 mm. In addition, Half Eagles were struck with a closed collar and beaded borders from that point onward. This modified format was continued from 1829 until the summer of 1834, at which time the Classic Head design was unveiled. This subtle change created not just one formidable rarity, but also another: the 1829 Large Planchet and 1829 Small Planchet Half Eagles. The two coins are comparable in overall scarcity; about eight exist of each variety, although forming an exact roster of known specimens is exceedingly difficult.

An incredible Gem Uncirculated 1829 Large Planchet Half Eagle was auctioned by Bowers and Merena Galleries in October 1999 as part of the Harry Bass collection. The coin was hammered down at $241,500—a record for the variety. A technically inferior 1829 Small Planchet Half Eagle was sold in the same auction for $80,500, a price more indicative of the individual coin's quality rather than the variety's desirability. The finest 1829 Small Planchet Half Eagle is the Byron Reed specimen, a beautiful Gem coin that sold for a remarkable $374,000 in 1996. Although opinions regarding its exact grade vary, it is undisputedly the finest example of the date and variety.

The reason for the Half Eagle size reduction in 1829 was to take advantage of new minting technologies. In particular, the "close" collar created perfectly uniform diameters by preventing the spread of the planchets allowed by the "loose" collar. The close collar also allowed for perfect centering of the dies on the planchet, yielding secondary benefits – a beaded border and a raised, circular rim. A "loose" collar required dies with borders that extended beyond the edges of the planchet, because the "loose" collar allowed some movement of the planchet beneath the dies. Thus, the often crude, tooth-like denticles gave way to the cleaner look of a circle of beads within a raised border.

1829 HALF EAGLE

Designed by John Reich. The obverse features a large head of Liberty surrounded by 13 stars with the date below. The reverse shows an eagle with spread wings, holding an olive branch and arrows. Surrounding the eagle are the inscriptions UNITED STATES OF AMERICA and 5 D., with the motto E PLURIBUS UNUM above the eagle's head. Standards: weight 8.75 grams; composition .916 gold/.083 silver; diameter 25 mm (large planchet) 23.8 mm (small planchet). Edge: reeded.

Rarity: Recent estimates suggest that eight Large Planchet specimens are known and an equal number of the Small Planchet variety. The rarity of the 1829 Half Eagles can be attributed to the massive meltings of early United States gold coins that occurred when their bullion value began to exceed their face value. In fact, some of the greatest American rarities, such as the 1815 and 1822 Half Eagles (both Top 100 coins) are siblings of the 1829 Half Eagles.

Photography courtesy Tom Mulvaney

Historical Value (Large)		
Uncirculated		
1960: $3,500 •	1980: $50,000 •	2003: $150,000

Historical Value (Small)		
Uncirculated		
1960: $3,500 •	1980: $45,000 •	2003: $125,000

To improve the design of U.S. coins, President Theodore Roosevelt personally sought the efforts of famed sculptor Augustus Saint-Gaudens. His works include some of the most important sculptures of the late nineteenth century. One of his most visible works is the *Sherman Victory* monument, a statuary group which stands in Grand Army Plaza at the southeast corner of New York's Central Park.

Roosevelt was a great admirer of classic Greek coins and wanted an American coinage of similar appearance. The president especially liked the high relief of the ancient coinage. Because of the difficulty in mass-producing high-relief coinage, Saint-Gaudens restricted his design work to the Ten Dollar and Double Eagle. The artist preferred the Indian Head design for the Double Eagle coinage. One Pattern coin of that design was struck at the artist's request, but eventually, the Indian Head design was chosen for the Ten Dollar gold coin, with examples of the new design struck in late 1907.

The first variety of the 1907 Ten Dollar Indian produced is the so-called "Wire Rim, With Period." Reportedly, 500 were struck and this design type is considered experimental per conventional wisdom, although research has revealed that, in fact, these were made as delicacies to be distributed by Mint officials, Treasury Department officials, and others. To acquire one at the time of issue, you needed a "connection"! Charles Barber, the Chief Engraver of the U.S. Mint, changed the design by giving the coin broad, raised borders, creating the so-called "Rolled Edge" type. According to Mint Director, Frank Leach, the Mint struck 31,500 pieces of this modified design on the coining press, and 50 examples were struck on the medal press. The large mintage is an important aspect of the 1907 "Rolled Edge" Ten Dollar. This clearly demonstrates that this issue was made for circulation and was not experimental. Although Charles Barber was happy with the new design, the Superintendent of the Mint, John Landis, was not. He preferred the final design, now known as the 1907 "No Periods." With the exception of 40-50 coins (which, again, were privately distributed by Mint and Treasury officials), all of the "Rolled Edge" coins were melted. Most surviving examples are Brilliant Gems. Several circulated coins are known, probably those that were saved as pocket-piece souvenirs. One certified Proof example exists and is possibly a survivor of the 50 examples that were struck on the medal press as related by Director Leach. The 1907 "Rolled Edge" Ten Dollar Indian is one of the most highly desired United States coins struck in the twentieth century.

Designed by Augustus Saint-Gaudens. The obverse displays the head of Liberty wearing an Indian headdress with 13 stars above the portrait. The reverse features a magnificent eagle perched on a bundle of arrows. Mintage for the issue is 31,550, but nearly all were melted. Standards: weight 16.718 grams; composition .900 gold/.100 copper; diameter 27 mm; net weight .48375 oz pure gold. Edge: displays 48 stars representing the states of the Union at the time.

Rarity: It is estimated that 35-45 Mint State examples remain in all grades. Although a few circulated coins are known, most survivors seen are Brilliant Gems. Only one certified Proof example is currently known to exist.

1907 "ROLLED EDGE" TEN DOLLARS

Historical Value		
Choice Uncirculated		
1960: $3,500	1980: $40,000	2003: $85,000

1933 TEN DOLLAR GOLD

The Philadelphia Mint struck 312,500 examples of the 1933 Ten Dollar gold coin. On March 6, 1933, however, President Franklin D. Roosevelt issued an order banning the private ownership of gold and marking the end of gold coin production in the United States. In response to the banking crisis in America and in an attempt to stimulate price and wage increases, the president eventually removed all gold coinage from the economy. Gold coinage had been produced on a nearly uninterrupted basis since 1795, though there were long periods of time, including 1821-1834 and 1861-1878, when gold coins were not seen in general circulation. Thus, 1933 became the last year for nearly 50 years that gold coins were produced in the United States. Double Eagles and Ten Dollar coins minted in Philadelphia constituted the only gold coinage for the year. The Ten Dollar coins were issued before the order banning private gold ownership became law. Until very recently, the 1933 Ten Dollar Eagle was the only gold coin struck that year which, according to a later position taken by the Treasury Department, was legal to own. Currently, the United States government has declared only one 1933 Double Eagle legal to own (see the 1933 Double Eagle). The year 1933 is historically important in American coinage, and the 1933 Eagle is a fascinating survivor of the era.

The original mintage of the 1933 Eagle was 312,500 pieces, well ahead of more than half the dates in the series, all of which are readily available and affordable today. However, once Roosevelt's order came down, virtually the entire stock of 1933 Eagles was destroyed, eventually being converted back into bullion and becoming a part of America's huge gold reserve (think Fort Knox). Thus, a date that might once have been common and pedestrian is now a great rarity and a Top 100 coin!

Designed by Augustus Saint-Gaudens. The obverse displays the head of Liberty wearing an Indian headdress with 13 stars above the portrait. The reverse features a magnificent eagle perched on a bundle of arrows. Mintage for the issue is 312,500, but nearly all were melted. Standards: weight 16.718 grams; composition .900 gold/.100 copper; diameter 27 mm; net weight .48375 oz pure gold. Edge: displays 48 stars representing the number of states of the Union at the time.

Rarity: As a result of the Presidential Order, nearly the entire mintage of 1933 Ten Dollar gold coins was melted. It is estimated that only 30-40 examples are known today. Most known examples are in Mint condition and were surely obtained directly from the Mint. A few Gem specimens are known to exist. The 1933 Gold Eagle is considered a great rarity and is particularly popular due to its intriguing year of issue.

1933 TEN DOLLARS

Photography courtesy David Akers & Tom Mulvaney

Historical Value		
Choice Uncirculated		
1960: $2,500	1980: $75,000	2003: $150,000

1848 "CAL" QUARTER EAGLE

The California Gold Rush began on January 24, 1848, when James Marshall discerned a gleaming gold nugget at Sutter's Mill on the American River. This had a profound impact on American numismatics, when one considers that a new mint was established in San Francisco (in 1854), and countless assayers and refiners began to strike their own coinage, and that the Double Eagle became a staple of America's currency system because of this gold discovery. One of the more interesting by-products of the Gold Rush is the 1848 CAL Quarter Eagle.

On December 9, 1848, California's military governor, Colonel R.B. Mason sent 230 ounces of the yellow metal to Secretary of War William L. Marcy. Secretary Marcy, in turn, had the bullion delivered to Philadelphia Mint Director Robert Maskell Patterson, who was instructed to use some of the gold for specially marked Quarter Eagles. 1,389 pieces were produced, all stamped with the abbreviation CAL. on the upper reverse, just above the Eagle's head, in commemoration of the important discovery in California. Due to this special inscription, many numismatists rightfully consider the 1848 CAL Quarter Eagles the nation's first commemorative coin.

Because the 1848 CAL Quarter Eagle was a direct result of the California Gold Rush, it is a highly coveted issue. Not only does the coin have a direct link to America history, but also it is one of the rarest regular-issue Liberty Head Quarter Eagles. Because many examples are deeply reflective, some old listings suggest that a few 1848 CAL Quarter Eagles were struck in Proof format. However, modern study has revealed that all were struck from the same pair of dies at the same time and that the dies had a Prooflike, not Proof, finish.

Apparently, the word "CAL." was punched into the dies while the coins were still in the press, preventing any flattening on the opposite side of the coin. At least one coin shows evidence of having been punched three times! All of the coins were stamped with the same punch, but the position of the punch sometimes varies. Nefarious individuals, wishing to capitalize on this rarity, have attempted to create counterfeits by making their own "CAL." punch and stamping it into the back of 1848 Quarter Eagles from Philadelphia. Fortunately, no one has yet been able to duplicate the "CAL." punch exactly, but certification of any 1848 "CAL." Quarter Eagle is a must.

Why just this one batch of Quarter Eagles was counter-stamped is a mystery. If the goal were to show the gold's origin, the same should have been done for the millions upon millions of gold coins created in later years from the steady stream of gold that flowed out of California.

Designed by Christian Gobrecht. The obverse features a figure of Liberty wearing a coronet. The word LIBERTY is inscribed on the headband. 13 stars encircle the portrait with the date at the bottom. The reverse depicts a spread eagle located in the center with the words UNITED STATES OF AMERICA written towards the edge. The denomination 2½ D. is featured at the base of the reverse. Standards: weight 4.18 grams; composition: .900 gold/.100 copper; diameter 18 mm. Edge: reeded.

Rarity: Fewer than 75 1848 CAL Quarter Eagles are believed to exist.

Historical Value
Uncirculated
1960: $1,500 • 1980: $20,000 • 2003: $45,000

Photography courtesy Mike Storeim

1842 "SMALL DATE" QUARTER DOLLAR

The 1842 "Small Date" Seated Liberty Quarter Dollar is a rarity known only in Proof condition and represented by five demonstrably different examples, plus a few other possibilities.

In the 1840s, Proof coins were sold individually or as part of complete sets. The opportunity to purchase Proof coins was not advertised by the Mint, nor were most collectors aware of the possibility. It was not until the late 1850s that the Mint standardized the regulations concerning the sale of Proof sets and began to make a regular business out of it (a similar situation occurred in the 1940s, when the Treasury tired of filling individual orders for Uncirculated coins and began offering official Mint Sets).

In the early 1940s, a complete set of copper and silver 1842 Proof coins was discovered in Connecticut by Oscar G. Schilke. The set contained a "Small Date" Quarter Dollar, which was later sold as an individual piece when the set was broken up. The 1842 Proof set assembled by the late John Jay Pittman, who acquired coins singly, contained an 1842 "Large Date" Quarter Dollar that turned out not to be a Proof, but a Proof-like Uncirculated piece. No Proof 1842 "Large Date" Quarter Dollar has ever come to light, nor are any expected because all of the Proofs are of the Small Date variety. Thus, in 1842, we find two major Quarter Dollar varieties: the Proof-only "Small Dates" and the Circulation strike-only "Large Dates."

Of the five known Proof 1842 "Small Date" Quarter Dollars, two are in institutional collections (the Smithsonian and the American Numismatic Society), the whereabouts of two of the examples are unknown, and the fifth example, from the celebrated Louis Eliasberg collection, resold in July 2002 for $87,400 (an $11,400 increase in just over five years).

1842 "SMALL DATE" QUARTER DOLLAR

The Quarter Dollar was not the only denomination to undergo changes in the size of the date in 1842. "Small Date" and "Large Date" varieties are known also for Large Cents, Half Dollars, Half Eagles, and Eagles, but none compare with the rarity of the 1842 "Small Date" Quarter Dollar (with the possible exception of the 1842 "Small Date, Small Letters" Half Dollar). Virtually every denomination was "tweaked" at some time in the 1840s, all with the goal of improving the coin and adding uniformity to its appearance. The success of this program was expressed in the long life of the Liberty Seated design on silver coins and the Coronet design on gold coins.

Designed by Christian Gobrecht. The obverse shows Miss Liberty in a flowing gown sitting on a rock. Her left hand holds a staff surmounted by a Liberty Cap; her right hand steadies a shield and holds a band bearing the word LIBERTY. 13 stars appear in an arc above Miss Liberty, and the date appears at the base of the obverse, below the rock. The reverse shows an eagle with a shield on its chest, an olive branch in its right talon, and a bunch of arrows in its left. The words UNITED STATES OF AMERICA appear above the eagle; the abbreviations QUAR. DOL. appear below. Standards: weight 103 grains; composition .900 silver/.100 copper; diameter 24.3 mm. Edge: reeded.

Rarity: Extremely Rare, struck only as Proofs in an extremely limited quantity. The finest 1842 "Small Date" Quarter Dollar appears to be the above-mentioned Eliasberg coin, an attractively toned Gem Proof.

Photography courtesy Doug Plasencia at Bowers and Merena Galleries

Historical Value		
Choice Proof		
1960: $2,500 •	1980: $15,000 •	2003: $85,000

One of the most beautiful and finely executed of all American coins is the 1792 Pattern Quarter Dollar.

The 1792 Pattern Quarter Dollar was created as part of a series of Pattern coins meant to pave the way for the regular production of coins in 1793. Unfortunately, no "real" Quarter Dollars were struck until 1796 and then with a completely different design. Credit for the design of the 1792 Pattern Quarter Dollar goes to Joseph Wright, an American artist who became the first engraver of the United States Mint. His delicate hand can also be seen on the Liberty Cap Large Cents issued in the last part of 1793. Unfortunately, Wright's tenure as engraver was cut short by Yellow Fever, a dreaded and deadly disease that afflicted Philadelphians in 1793 and several years thereafter. Both Wright and his wife died in 1793, just as the Mint was finding its footing.

For many years, the 1792 Pattern Quarter Dollar remained a mystery because, unlike all of the other 1792 Patterns, this one bore no markings as to its intended denomination or value. At various times and by various numismatists, this has been called a Pattern Cent, Pattern Quarter Dollar, or Pattern Half Eagle.

The confusion is justified. The diameter of the 1792 Pattern Quarter Dollar matches closely that of the first Cents made in 1793, but the edge reeding indicates that the intent was to produce a coin of gold or silver (copper coins had lettered or ornamented edges). The diameter was also similar to (but slightly larger than) that of the first Half Eagles. The combination of an eagle reverse with no denomination made a tempting comparison.

Contemporary evidence revealed the true intention behind these coins. Before his death, Wright asked his neighbor to submit a bill to the Mint for work he had performed on "Two Essays of a Quarter Dollar . . . " The only coin that could possibly fit the evidence is the 1792 Pattern Quarter Dollar.

1792 Pattern Quarter Dollar are found in a variety of different metals and formats, including normal-sized copper pieces, over-sized white metal (pewter?) examples, and one-sided examples in white metal. All of them are either extremely rare or unique.

Designed by Joseph Wright. The obverse shows a delicate bust of Miss Liberty facing right, her hair tied up neatly with a ribbon. The word LIBERTY hovers above her head and the date appears beneath. The border is a simple raised circle. The reverse features an eagle with outstretched wings standing on a round mound (globe?) surrounded by UNITED STATES OF AMERICA. The border consists of 87 tiny stars. Standards: weight 175-180 grains for copper, 400+ grains for white metal; diameter 28 mm or larger; metal content either pure copper or white metal. Edge: reeded on the normal-sized pieces; plain on the over-sized examples.

Rarity: Extremely Rare. Only two copper examples are known, the finest of which is in the National Numismatic Collection at the Smithsonian Institution. Two white metal pieces are known as well as a pair of uniface white metal pieces.

1792 PATTERN
QUARTER DOLLAR

Photography courtesy Smithsonian Institution and Douglas Mudd

Historical Value		
Extremely Fine		
1960: $2,500	1980: $30,000	2003: $175,000

Only seven examples of the 1817/4 Half Dollar are known, earning it the title of "King of the Capped Bust Half Dollars" and making it one of the rarest of all United States Coins.

The 1817/4 Half Dollar illustrates the conservative economics of the early United States Mint by showing how old dies were turned into "new" ones simply by changing the last digit of the date. Although there were many exceptions, it was the general policy to strike coins only in the year shown on the die. By 1815, at least three Half Dollar dies were left over: one from 1812, a second from 1813, and a third from 1814. In preparation for striking 1815 Half Dollars, the engraver grabbed the oldest die (the 1812) and stamped a 5 over the 2. This die was then used to strike Half Dollars, all of which show a clear overdate.

In 1816, no Half Dollars were struck because of a fire at the Mint that destroyed some of the machinery. In 1817, after repairs were made and production of Half Dollars was ready to resume, the engraver pulled out the two 1813 and 1814 dies and punched a 7 in the place of the last digits, creating two overdates for the year. The 1817/3 die performed well, turning out enough coins that the variety is readily available today. On the other hand, the 1817/4 die broke quickly, cracking nearly in half while producing an unknown (but obviously small) number of coins.

The 1817/4 Half Dollar is so rare that it remained unknown to collectors until 1930, when E.T. Wallis of Los Angeles, California, announced the discovery in a full-page advertisement on the back of one of his auction sale catalogs. A second example turned up sometime between 1940 and 1942, mistakenly sold as one of the "Punctuated Date" varieties. Subsequent discoveries occurred in the early 1960s, another of which was a misattributed "Punctuated Date." A seventh example was discovered in 1976. No more 1817/4 Half Dollars have been found since then (although you can rest assured that every specialist and knowledgeable dealer is looking for them)!

Designed by John Reich. The obverse features a bust of Liberty wearing a freedman's cap with the word LIBERTY on the band. 13 stars circle the bust; the date appears on the bottom of the obverse. The reverse features an eagle, with open wings and a shield on its chest, holding an olive branch and a bundle of arrows. A scroll with the words E PLURIBUS UNUM hovers above the eagle. UNITED STATES OF AMERICA appears near the rim; the denomination 50 C sits beneath the eagle. Standards: weight 208 grains; composition .892 silver/.108 copper; diameter 32 mm. Edge: lettered FIFTY CENTS OR HALF A DOLLAR with a star between DOLLAR and FIFTY.

Rarity: Seven known. The finest 1817/4 Half Dollar is the coin from the Louis Eliasberg collection (the only complete collection of United States coins ever formed). This particular coin was graded Extremely Fine-45 in the 1997 sale of Eliasberg's silver coins, where it reached the princely sum of $209,000. Subsequently, the coin received a grade of About Uncirculated-50 from the Professional Coin Grading Service.

Photography courtesy Sheridan Downey

GREATEST U.S. COINS

Historical Value		
Extremely Fine		
1960: $3,500	1980: $40,000	2003: $200,000

1853-O "NO ARROWS" HALF DOLLAR

Only three examples of the 1853-O Seated Liberty Half Dollar "Without Arrows and Rays" are known today. While this number is extremely low, one might also consider it extremely high, considering that Mint records indicate that none were struck!

The story of this rarity begins with the Mint Act of February 21, 1853, which reduced the weight of the Half Dollars from 206 grains to 192 grains. In order to make the public aware of this change, special features were added to the lighter weight coins; arrowheads were placed on either side of the date and rays were placed around the eagle on the reverse. These marks made it easy for the government and the public to identify the new coins and to differentiate them from the older, heavier coins that were worth more than their face value. Many millions of the older coins were melted down and converted into lighter weight coins or bullion. Thus, the survival of any pre-1853 silver coin depended on coin collectors (few in number at the time), hoarders, and just plain luck.

In late 1852 or early 1853, the New Orleans Mint received a shipment of dies from the Philadelphia Mint, just as it did every year, to prepare for the new year's coinage. These dies bore no arrowheads on either side of the date, nor rays on the reverse. Quite possibly, the New Orleans Mint struck a quantity of 1853-O Half Dollars with no arrows or rays early in 1853, before the new Mint Act went into effect. Presumably, they were all destroyed (or were believed to have been destroyed) after the effective date of the Act, thus explaining why none are recorded in the Mint's records.

Regardless of how, when, or why they were made, 1853-O Half Dollars without the arrowheads or rays most certainly exist.

Had the law not been changed in 1853, the 1853-O "No Arrows" Half Dollar would be a very common coin, indeed, as indicated by the one-million-plus mintage of the 1853-O "With Arrows" Half Dollar. However, such are the twists of fate through which great rarities are born. Often, the difference between being "common" and "rare" hinges on a single circumstance; other times, rarity is caused by a number of factors occurring at the same time. Yes, rarities are sometimes deliberate creations (1913 Liberty Head Nickel or any of the 1866 "No Motto" Silver Coins). The purist, however, would argue that the most important rarities are those, like the 1853-O "No Arrows" Half Dollar, that occurred as naturally as possible.

Designed by Christian Gobrecht. The obverse shows Miss Liberty in a flowing gown sitting on a rock. Her left hand holds a staff surmounted by a Liberty Cap; her right hand steadies a shield and holds a band bearing the word LIBERTY. 13 stars appear in an arc above Miss Liberty and the date appears at the base of the obverse, below the rock. The reverse shows an eagle with a shield on its chest, an olive branch in its right talon, and a bunch of arrows in its left. The words UNITED STATES OF AMERICA appear above the eagle; the abbreviation HALF. DOL. appears below. Standards: weight 206 grains; composition .900 silver/.100 copper; diameter 30 mm. Edge: reeded.

Rarity: Extremely Rare. Only three 1853-O "No Arrows" Half Dollars are known to exist. The finest example is Very Fine; the others grade only Good and Very Good.

1853-O "NO ARROWS"
HALF DOLLAR

Photography courtesy Stack's

Historical Value		
	Fine	
1960: $3,500	1980: $25,000	2003: $175,000

In 1916, Hermon MacNeil redesigned the Quarter Dollar as part of an on-going effort begun in 1905 by then-President Theodore Roosevelt to bring a fresh look to all American coins. Unfortunately, MacNeil's look was a bit too fresh; his vision included a partially nude Miss Liberty, a first on any American coin struck for circulation. MacNeil's risqué design was modified in 1917, when Miss Liberty was given a chaste coat of mail with which to cover herself. Early conventional wisdom was that the coverup was due to a prudish outcry against nudity. Today, however, it is thought that the change was made to depict Miss Liberty ready for defense, or for war—with the World War raging in Europe since August 1914.

The redesign of the Quarter Dollar should not have taken place until 1917, due to a federal law making it illegal to change coinage designs more than once every twenty-five years. The Barber Quarter Dollar debuted in 1892 and was slated for retirement no earlier than the end of 1916. However, the decision was made to implement MacNeil's new design at the end of 1916, when 52,000 examples were struck for circulation. Little or no notice was given that Quarter Dollars of the new design had been struck, and before anyone knew it, virtually the entire mintage was released into circulation. As a result, Uncirculated examples of the 1916 Standing Liberty Quarter Dollar are very scarce today.

Having itself already "broken" the law prohibiting designs changes more than once every 25 years, the Standing Liberty Quarter Dollar fell victim to its own set of special circumstances. In 1932, a Quarter Dollar commemorating the 200th anniversary of the birth of George Washington replaced the design, supposedly for one year only. Unfortunately, the new Washington Quarter Dollar was so popular that it was continued as a regular issue coin, thereby completely replacing the Standing Liberty design after only fifteen years!

Designed by Hermon MacNeil. The obverse shows a full-length view of a partially nude Miss Liberty in a flowing gown. She holds a shield in her left hand and an olive branch in her right and appears to be walking through some sort of gate, emblazoned with IN GOD WE TRUST and stars. The word LIBERTY appears in an arc at the top of the obverse, and the date appears beneath Liberty's feet. The reverse shows an eagle in flight. The legends UNITED STATES OF AMERICA and E PLURIBUS UNUM appear above the eagle; QUARTER DOLLAR appears beneath. 13 stars are divided in their arrangement on the reverse (seven to the left of the eagle and six to the right). Standards: weight 96 grains; composition .900 silver/.100 copper; diameter 24.3 mm. Edge: reeded.

Rarity: 52,000 struck for circulation, plus an estimated five Proofs. A few hundred Uncirculated examples are known, most of which fall into the MS-62 to MS-64 grade levels. Above MS-65, the 1916 Standing Liberty Quarter Dollar becomes extremely rare; Superb pieces are virtually non-existent.

Photography courtesy Tom Mulvaney

Historical Value
Choice Uncirculated
1960: $750 • 1980: $2,500 • 2003: $7,500

1851-O SILVER DOLLAR

Most collectors (and even seasoned professional dealers) have never even heard of the unique 1851-O Silver Dollar. This is not surprising given the coin is not listed in most reference books, including Walter Breen's monumental *Complete Encyclopedia of U.S. & Colonial Coins*. As with several of the Top 100 coins, there are no Mint records to support the existence of the 1851-O Silver Dollar. One might also ask, "Why is there only one?"

The coin itself presents a bit of an enigma. The mint mark on the reverse is weak and scraped, indicating an attempt to erase it from the coin. Because of the unusual situation centering on the mint mark, two theories have developed to explain the existence of this otherwise inexplicable coin.

The first theory suggests that the coin was struck sometime around 1858-1860, during a time when other American rarities were being restruck. Certainly, additional Proof 1851 Dollars (another Top 100 coin) were being restruck around the same time, as well as other rarities such as the 1804 Silver Dollar and the 1852 Silver Dollar. Proponents of this theory claim that a Silver Dollar of undetermined date previously struck at the New Orleans Mint (thus bearing an "O" mint mark) was used as the planchet for a Restrike 1851 Silver Dollar. This would have resulted in a flattened mint mark. To confirm this theory, the coin may show additional, telltale marks, such as the undertype of another date below the 1851. In support of this theory, the coin has been certified as a Proof-62, which would not be the case if it were a genuine circulation strike from the New Orleans Mint in 1851.

The second theory, a bit far-fetched, acknowledges that the 1851-O Silver Dollar was indeed made much later than the date on the coin, but that it was a case of mistaken identity where the fabricators accidentally created a previously unknown coin by mulling the front of an 1851 Silver Dollar with the back of a New Orleans Mint Dollar (remember that the Philadelphia Mint was responsible for preparing the reverse dies – the ones with the mint marks – for the 1859-O and 1860-O Silver Dollars). Upon realizing their mistake, the "minters" made their best effort at flattening and removing the mint mark. Unfortunately for them (fortunately for coin collectors), they failed.

Regardless of the true status of this coin, the market has embraced it enthusiastically. In 2000, the coin was bid to $161,000 in its first-ever auction appearance, failing to meet the seller's reserve. With the proper publicity and recognition, the value of the 1851-O Silver Dollar could approach the half million dollar mark.

Designed by Christian Gobrecht. The obverse shows Miss Liberty in a flowing gown sitting on a rock. Her left hand holds a staff surmounted by a Liberty Cap; her right hand steadies a shield and holds a band bearing the word LIBERTY. 13 stars appear in an arc around Miss Liberty, and the date appears at the base of the obverse, below the rock. The reverse shows an eagle with a shield on its chest, an olive branch in its right talon, and a bunch of arrows in its left. The words UNITED STATES OF AMERICA appear above the eagle; the abbreviation ONE DOL. appears below. Standards: weight 26.7 grams; composition .900 silver/.100 copper; diameter 38 mm. Edge: reeded.

Rarity: Unique!

1851-O SILVER DOLLAR

Historical Value		
Choice Proof		
1960: N/A	1980: N/A	2003: $250,000

Of the 3,060 Half Dimes struck in 1802, only about 50 have survived. Until the discovery of the unique 1870-S Half Dime in 1978, the 1802 ruled the roost as "King" of the Half Dime series.

The story of the 1802 Half Dime is the classic story of attrition. Here's a coin that started out with a very low mintage, most of which was decimated over time as coins were lost or destroyed through various silver melts. The first appearance of an 1802 Half Dime at public auction was not until 1859 (even then, the condition of the coin was listed as "Poor"). By 1863, only three 1802 Half Dimes were known to exist. However, once the spotlight focused on this rarity, more examples began to appear. By 1883, 16 different examples were known. In the 1930s, dealer James G. Macallister claimed he knew of 35 examples. Today, the total population has risen to approximately 40-50 different examples. Certainly, a few others may exist in as-yet-undiscovered collections, but the rate that new discoveries are being made has slowed dramatically.

Despite listings of Uncirculated examples in old auction catalogs, no truly Mint State 1802 Half Dimes are known to exist. At least two examples have been certified at the About Uncirculated level, both of which had been called Uncirculated in the past. Most 1802 Half Dimes are found in low grade, often bent or battered.

The difficulty in determining the exact population of the 1802 Half Dimes illustrates the problems researchers encounter using old action records. Tracking a coin by its grade is useless because of the evolution of grading standards and terminology over the years. For instance, a Very Good coin from 100 years ago may be Very Fine today, and vice versa. Despite the promises of "standardized" grading, the simple truth is that even certified coins are broken out, re-submitted, and often re-graded at a different level. Tracking a coin by its photograph is also dangerous because, in some instances, coins (even important ones) were not plated at all and, in other instances, stock photographs were used over and over again to illustrate the type of coin, not the actual coin. Thus, today's researcher must rely instead on new tools such as scanning technologies, the Internet, computers, and more sophisticated (and better written) auction catalogs.

On average, collectors can expect to see but one 1802 Half Dime appear at auction in any given year. This means that the collector seeking to acquire one of these rarities must be patient, yet ready to act quickly, or wait a year for another one!

Ownership of any 1802 Half Dime is a mark of distinction and an accomplishment that many big "name" collectors failed to achieve.

Designed by Robert Scot. The obverse features a draped bust of Liberty with some of her hair tied back in a bow. LIBERTY appears above, the date below, and 13 stars are divided up on the sides (seven on the left, six on the right). The reverse features an heraldic eagle with outstretched wings (similar to that seen on the Great Seal of the United States). In its beak, the eagle holds a scroll with the words E PLURIBUS UNUM. In its left talon, the eagle grasps an olive branch; in its right talon, it holds a bunch of arrows. Clouds and 13 stars appear above the eagle. The outer legend reads: UNITED STATES OF AMERICA. No denomination appears anywhere on the coin. Standards: weight 21 grains; composition .892 silver/.108 copper; diameter 16.5 mm. Edge: reeded.

Rarity: Extremely Rare. Less than 50 1802 Half Dimes are known, the finest of which is a single AU-55.

1802 HALF DIME

Photography courtesy David Akers & Tom Mulvaney

Historical Value		
Extremely Fine		
1960: $2,000	1980: $25,000	2003: $75,000

1796 HALF CENTS – WITH AND WITHOUT POLE

Nearly every series of United States coins contains a classic rarity – in Half Cents, it's the 1796.

The mintage for the 1796 Half Cent is a mere 1,390 pieces. Compare this to the 139,690 Half Cents bearing the 1795 date and the 128,840 from 1797. Why were so few Half Cents made in 1796? The answer has to do with the availability of copper and the allocation of the resources available at the Mint.

In the early years of the U.S. Mint, finding copper for Half Cents and Large Cents was a constant problem. Native sources of copper were as yet largely untapped, and smelting operations in America were virtually non-existent. Thus, the Mint resorted to unorthodox (but ingenious) methods of procuring planchets (blanks) for its coins. In April 1795, the Mint purchased 1,076 pounds of cent-size copper tokens already stamped with the advertising message of Talbot, Allum & Lee, merchants of New York City. These were cut down in size and used to produce 1795 Half Cents. The Mint also made use of mis-struck or defective Large Cents, which were similarly cut down, then stamped with Half Cent dies. Often, Half Cents dated from 1795-1797 show portions of the designs of the original Talbot, Allum & Lee tokens and, less often, Large Cents.

Once the Talbot, Allum & Lee tokens were used on the 1795 Half Cents, there was no copper, except for a few spoiled Cents, with which to make 1796 Half Cents. Fortunately, the additional purchase of a small quantity of sheet copper from a local source enabled the Mint to strike some 1796 Half Cents.

Regarding the allocation of resources, by 1796 the Mint had already turned its attention to more lofty coins. Instead of worrying about copper for Half Cents, the Mint focused its attention on introducing three new denominations: the Dime, Quarter Dollar, and Quarter Eagle ($2.50 Gold) and on producing the bedrocks of America's monetary system, the Large Cent and Silver Dollar (in fact, 1796 was the first year that the Mint produced every possible denomination under the system then in place). With the attention focused on producing this wide variety of coins, scant effort was exerted on producing 1796 Half Cents.

Two varieties of the 1796 Half Cent exist: the normal version and another, unfinished version that lacks the staff that normally supports the Liberty Cap (this variety also features a heavy, nearly horizontal crack that bisects the front of the coin). Not surprisingly, the two varieties are known as the 1796 "With Pole" and "Without Pole" Half Cents. Both are very rare, the "Without Pole" variety being the rarer of the two.

Designed by Robert Scot, engraved by John Smith Gardner. The obverse features a bust of Liberty facing right, her hair flowing loosely behind her head. A Liberty Cap and supporting pole appear behind her head. LIBERTY appears above the bust, the date below. The reverse shows the words HALF CENT within a plain wreath, the fraction "1/200" below and UNITED STATES OF AMERICA surrounding. Standards: weight 84 grains; composition pure copper; diameter 23.5 mm. Edge: plain.

Rarity: Very Rare (With Pole) or Extremely Rare (No Pole). An unusually high percentage of 1796 Half Cents are known in excellent condition, including several Uncirculated examples. This may indicate that their rarity was recognized early on by collectors, who deliberately set aside nice examples, or that a small hoard may have been preserved accidentally. In any event, a nice Uncirculated 1796 Half Cent holds the record for the most valuable U.S. copper coin ever sold at auction - $506,000!

1796 HALF CENTS WITH POLE

Photography courtesy Tom Mulvaney

Historical Value (With Pole)		
Very Fine		
1960: $750	1980: $7,500	2003: $25,000

Historical Value (No Pole)		
Very Fine		
1960: $1,250	1980: $15,500	2003: $75,000

The idea for this unusual, internationally denominated Pattern came from Dana Bickford, who, upon his return from a trip abroad, proposed that America needed a coin that could be easily converted into the currencies of other nations. Bickford, an entrepreneur who devised many products including hand-operated knitting machines, believed that travelers needed an easy way to convert money as they traveled from country to country. The back of "Dana Bickford's International Coin," as it was called in 1876, bore the weight of the coin (in gold), the fineness (or purity), plus the value in six different international currencies. Unfortunately, because of the ever-changing relationship of world currencies, the "Bickford" Pattern proved unworkable and "died on the vine." Examples are known in a variety of metals, including two in gold.

At one time, the Bickford "Ten" was only known in copper. The two known gold examples are thought to have been part of the enormous trade of Patterns between A.L. Snowden and William Woodin as payment for the return of the 1877 Half Unions that are also discussed in this book. The gold Pattern coins were later included in the illustrious collections of Brand, Boyd, Wilson, and others. Both specimens were a part of the fabulous Wilkison collection of gold Patterns that was sold to Paramount International Coin Corporation in 1973.

The concept of a truly international coin continues to intrigue politicians and economists alike. The "Stellas" of 1879 and 1880 were failed attempts at an international coin, partly because the coins didn't really fit into our own coinage system. Today's Euro is perhaps the most successful international coin, allowing travelers to move from country to country within the European Union without having to change currencies or convert the prices of goods and services. However, as in 1874 and 1879 (and even today), any international coin is doomed to eventual failure because human nature favors competition over cooperation.

1874 BICKFORD TEN DOLLAR GOLD PATTERN

Designed by Dana Bickford and William Barber. The obverse has the head of Liberty facing left with a coronet bearing the word LIBERTY, inscribed below six stars. The reverse has a continuous rope divided into six sections with a conversion of various world currencies. Standards: weight 258 grains; composition gold; diameter 34 mm. Edge: reeded.

Rarity: Two examples are known in gold. Beware of deceptive copies from unofficial modern dies.

Photography courtesy Rarities LLC & Tom Mulvaney

Historical Value		
Choice Proof		
1960: $3,500	1980: $100,000	2003: $350,000

The 1861-D is the second rarest Gold Dollar, superseded only by the 1849-C Open Wreath. Though it is an undeniably scarce coin, its primary claim to fame is that it was struck under Confederate control. The same Congressional Act of 1835 that created the Charlotte Mint also established the Dahlonega Mint. Like its Charlotte counterpart, the Dahlonega Mint opened in 1838, striking only Quarter Eagles and Half Eagles. Though it was fairly prosperous in the 1840s and 1850s, the future of the Dahlonega Mint became uncertain in 1861. After the Confederacy took over the Mint in April of that year, director George Kellogg resigned and turned the facility over to the CSA. Using what limited bullion remained, rebel forces struck approximately 1,000-1,500 Gold Dollars in May of 1861.

The rebel minters were amateurs and obviously inexperienced. The quality of the Gold Dollars they struck was poor, as the strike was incomplete and the planchets were sloppily prepared. While most of the coins they struck were released into circulation, a small quantity was likely retained by the rebels. This accounts for the high number of Mint State survivors; almost all Dahlonega Gold Dollars are found well worn and battered from use. In total, approximately 50-60 of the original 1,000-1,500 pieces struck are known. Although the Dahlonega Mint also struck Half Eagles in 1861, these were probably minted early in the year under the auspices of Kellogg. The Gold Dollars, conversely, were clearly produced by rebels after the Union employees fled. This makes the 1861-D Gold Dollar unique as the only U.S. coin struck by rebels, for which no federal counterpart exists (in contrast, some 1861-O silver Half Dollars and some 1861-C Half Eagles were struck under federal auspices, others after the mints fell into the hands of the Confederacy).

The 1861-D Gold Dollar has been a favorite among collectors since the late nineteenth century. When the Gold Dollar denomination was discontinued in 1889, it became popular to try to form complete sets of the denomination. As numismatists began to collect the series, the 1861-D emerged as a challenging coin to acquire. When a specimen did appear at auction, bidding was always fierce and competitive. While the 1861-D Gold Dollar is not the most valuable coin discussed in this text, its connection to the Confederacy makes it one of the most historically significant.

Designed by James B. Longacre. The obverse features a head of LIBERTY wearing a feathered headdress. The word LIBERTY is inscribed on the headband. The legend UNITED STATES OF AMERICA is engraved at the perimeter. The reverse features the denomination 1 DOLLAR, and a wreath of corn and grain encircles the date. Standards: weight: 1.672 grams; composition .900 gold/.100 copper; diameter 15 mm. Edge: finely reeded.

Rarity: Between 50 to 60 coins exist, though some authors suggest that even fewer have survived.

Photography courtesy Hancock & Harwell and Tom Mulvaney

Historical Value		
Uncirculated		
1960: $2,000	1980: $15,000	2003: $35,000

Though the 1916-D Dime is no great rarity, it remains one of the most popular coins of the twentieth century, thus warranting inclusion as one of the Top 100 greatest American coins.

The story of the 1916-D Dime began over a decade earlier, when President Theodore Roosevelt ordered the redesign of all American coins. Gold coins underwent facelifts in 1907 and 1908, the Cent in 1909, and the Nickel in 1913. The Dime, Quarter Dollar, and Half Dollar were forced to wait until 1916 because a law required coin designs to be in place for 25 years before they could be changed.

Adolph A. Weinman was chosen to redesign the Dime and Half Dollar. For the Dime, Weinman chose a head of Liberty wearing a winged cap. The artist intended for the wings to represent freedom of thought, but because so many people confused the image with the Roman messenger-god, Mercury, the coin became known popularly as the "Mercury Head" Dime.

In keeping with tradition, the Philadelphia Mint bore the brunt of Dime production in 1916, followed closely by the San Francisco Mint. The third Mint (at Denver) was hardly a factor in 1916, producing only 264,000 Dimes, barely one hundredth of the Dimes produced at Philadelphia. This tiny mintage was to be the lowest of any Mercury Head Dime produced from the beginning of the series in 1916 until the demise of the design in 1945.

1916-D MERCURY DIME

Thus, it's easy to understand why this date has become so popular with collectors; every school-kid in America needed the date to complete a set. Even when silver coins were still in circulation, the 1916-D Dime seemed to be the one date that could not be found in loose change. Nevertheless, most 1916-D Dimes known today are well worn, indicating that the scarcity of this date was not initially recognized. Indeed, finding a nice Very Fine or better example is difficult (and expensive).

Designed by A.A. Weinman. The obverse features a head of Liberty wearing a winged cap, LIBERTY above, IN GOD WE TRUST at lower left, and the date below the bust. The reverse shows a fasces (ax and bundle of sticks tied together) in front of an olive branch, UNITED STATES OF AMERICA in an arc above, ONE DIME in an arc below, E PLURIBUS UNUM in the right field. Standards: weight 2.50 grams; composition .900 silver/.100 copper; diameter 18 mm. Edge: reeded.

Rarity: Scarce. The true scarcity of the 1916-D Dime has been masked by the presence of numerous fakes, most of which were created by the addition of a small mint mark on the back of a Philadelphia Dime. Certification remains a must to prevent the disappointment of discovering, sometimes years later, that your beloved 1916-D Dime is an impostor!

Photography courtesy Tom Mulvaney

Historical Value		
Choice Uncirculated		
1960: $750	• 1980: $3,500	• 2003: $10,000

The 1895 Silver Dollar is known as the "King of the Morgan Dollars" and is usually the last coin that collectors need to complete their sets.

Mint records show that 12,000 1895 Dollars were made for circulation and 880 Proofs were made for sale to collectors at a premium. If the mintage figure of 12,000 pieces were correct, the 1895 Dollar would be by far the rarest of any Morgan Silver Dollar (the only other dates that come close are the 1893-S and 1894, both with mintages of 100,000 or above). However, the mintage figure is not correct, making the 1895 Silver Dollar much rarer than it appears even at first glance. Either the 12,000 figure is an accounting entry for coins of another year, likely 1894, or the 12,000 1895 Silver Dollars are hidden away somewhere, as no "circulation strike" has ever been seen. The several 1895 Dollars that are worn are all believed to be Proofs that escaped into circulation. A true Uncirculated 1895 Silver Dollar would be one of the greatest finds in numismatic history.

Because of the great demand for this date, prices for 1895 Silver Dollars are considerably higher than for Proofs of other dates of comparable mintage. For instance, a Gem Proof 1895 Dollar trades in the $25,000-$30,000 range while Gem Proofs of most other dates sell in the $5,000-$6,000 range.

Such is the price of popularity!

Designed by George Morgan. The obverse features a large head of Miss Liberty facing left, wearing a freedman's cap banded with the word LIBERTY and a wreath of American agricultural produce. E PLURIBUS UNUM appears in an arc around Liberty's head; the date appears below. 13 stars are divided on either side of the obverse (seven on the left and six on the right). The reverse features a plain eagle with wings raised and outstretched, holding an olive branch and arrows in its talons. IN GOD WE TRUST appears above the eagle in script. A wreath arcs around below the eagle and the legends UNITED STATES OF AMERICA and ONE DOLLAR appear in a circular arrangement on the outside of the coin. Standards: weight 26.7 grams; composition .900/ silver/.100 copper; diameter 38 mm. Edge: reeded.

Rarity: Rare. A surprising number of circulated Proof 1895 Silver Dollars exist, by some estimates as many as 50-75. As "common" as the circulated Proofs are, none have sold for less than $12,000 in recent years, which is almost as much as some of the Proof-60 and better pieces have brought. Most examples fall in the Proof-62 to Proof-64 category. Gems are scarce and Superb examples are extremely rare. A couple of incredibly beautiful Proof-68 examples are known; these always turn heads and fetch record prices whenever they appear on the market.

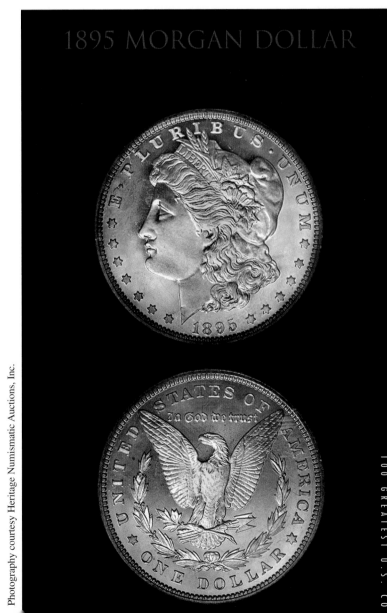

Photography courtesy Heritage Numismatic Auctions, Inc.

Historical Value		
Choice Proof		
1960: $1,500	1980: $17,500	2003: $25,000

1796 "NO STARS" QUARTER EAGLE

When the founding fathers created America's coinage system in 1792, three gold denominations were included: the Quarter Eagle, Half Eagle, and Eagle. However, demand for high-denomination coins was extremely limited. With the average worker making only a few dollars per week, one can imagine how infrequently large coins were used. Whereas the first copper coins were produced in 1793 and silver coins in 1794, it was not until 1795 that the Philadelphia Mint began to strike gold coins. The Quarter Eagle, in fact, was not introduced until 1796. The dies had already been prepared, possibly as early as 1795, but there was no demand until the summer of 1796.

The 1796 "No Stars" Quarter Eagle is known mostly for its unusual obverse design. All 1796-dated gold and silver coins display stars on the front, with the sole exception of the "No Stars" Quarter Eagle. The reason for this remains uncertain. Some have suggested that the star punch used to engrave the dies broke. Another theory is that the Mint employees were reluctant to engrave the stars because new states were in the process of being admitted (for a while, the number of stars on American coins directly corresponded with the number of states in the Union). With some states still in limbo, perhaps the Mint did not want to put an inaccurate number of stars on the coin.

Later in 1796, the Philadelphia Mint struck an updated version of the Quarter Eagle featuring 16 stars on the obverse. After striking 963 pieces without stars, the Mint produced an additional 432 with the traditional stars. Even though the "With Stars" variety is significantly scarcer, the "No Stars" version has always been more popular. In 1995, the finest known 1796 "No Stars" Quarter Eagle was sold in a New York auction. After fierce bidding, the coin was hammered down for $602,000. A good argument could be made proclaiming that coin as the most desirable eighteenth-century gold coin. Not only is it rare but also it is the only year this design was produced.

The question of how many stars to place on coins was a common one in the early years of the Mint. Initially, the goal was to honor the original 13 colonies; after all, their group had mustered the nerve to band together and break away from and defeat the British Empire. Thereafter, it was felt that each new state should be honored with its own star. However, the rule does not seem to have been applied consistently; engravers sometimes forgot to add an extra star or they may simply have run out of room on the dies. By 1798, the question appears to have been settled in favor of 13 stars, but that was not necessarily the end of any mistakes. The 1817 "15 Stars" Large Cent and 1828 "12 Stars" Half Cent (neither of which are rare enough to make the Top 100) are glaring examples of how easily mistakes can be made.

Which American coin features the largest number of stars? The 1839 "Starry Field Reverse" Gobrecht Dollar is a candidate with 39 stars, but the real winner is the 1794 "Starred Reverse" Large Cent, with 94 (coincidentally, one for each year)!

Designed by Robert Scot. The obverse features Miss Liberty wearing a cap or turban. The word LIBERTY is featured at the top with the date located at the bottom. The reverse depicts an eagle surrounded by the words UNITED STATES OF AMERICA. Above the eagle's head is a field of stars and six clouds. Standards: weight: 4.37 grams; composition .916 gold/.083 copper; diameter 20 mm. Edge: reeded.

Rarity: The exact number of specimens known is often debated. At least 100 coins survived, although there is the possibility that as many as 200 exist.

1796 "NO STARS" QUARTER EAGLE

Photography courtesy Tom Mulvaney

Historical Value		
About Uncirculated		
1960: $2,500	1980: $20,000	2003: $75,000

Like the 1796 Half Dollar (another Top 100 coin), the 1797 Half Dollar is a classic American rarity. The mintages of the 1796 and 1797 Half Dollars were co-mingled in the Mint records, and the total number of coins for both dates is a mere 3,918 pieces. Factor in the coins that were lost or destroyed, and the number of survivors becomes significantly small.

In 1797, the Mint produced a full complement of legal denominations except for one: the Quarter Dollar. At the time, depositors of silver bullion at the Mint could request the denomination(s) desired, and most requests were for Silver Dollars, to the detriment of Half Dollars.

1797 was the last year of the Plain (or Small) Eagle reverse. This pitiful looking bird was replaced in 1801 with a more impressive and intimidating Heraldic Eagle borrowed from the Great Seal of the United States.

Most 1797 Half Dollars known today are well circulated. Collectors are willing to accept examples in just about any grade, including coins that have been professionally repaired (holes filled, scratches removed), coins they would not accept were the 1797 Half Dollar more available. A few Uncirculated 1797 Half Dollars are known to exist, but they are not as common as Mint State 1796 Half Dollars, nor do they come as nice. For instance, the finest 1797 Half Dollar rates a grade of MS-63, while there are a couple of 1796 Half Dollars at that grade and higher.

Curiously, the Draped Bust, Small Eagle Reverse Half Dollar (a two-year type of which the 1797 is a member) was the first Silver American coin to bear a denomination on the reverse, despite that the denomination was already stated by the edge lettering. The practice was not carried over when the design of the Half Dollar changed in 1801. Denominations first appeared on the reverse of silver coins in the following order: 1809 for Dimes, 1815 for Quarter Dollars, 1829 for Half Dimes, 1836 for Silver Dollars, and 1851 for Three-Cents Silver!

Designed by Robert Scot. The obverse features a draped bust of Liberty with some of her hair tied back in a bow. LIBERTY appears above, the date below, and stars are divided up on the sides (one variety has 15 stars, the other has 16 stars). The reverse features a plain eagle standing on clouds with outstretched wings within a wreath of palm and olive branches. The outer legend reads UNITED STATES OF AMERICA. The denomination appears as the fraction "1/2" beneath the bow of the wreath. Standards: weight 208 grains; composition .892 silver/.108 copper; diameter 32.5 mm. Edge: lettered FIFTY CENTS OR HALF A DOLLAR.

Rarity: The mintage of 1797 Half Dollars is unknown but is most certainly small. The total mintage of all 1796 and 1797 amounted to only 3,918 coins! Mint State examples are extremely rare and rate MS-63 at best.

1797 HALF DOLLAR

Photography courtesy John Hamrick

Historical Value		
Extremely Fine		
1960: $2,000	1980: $15,000	2003: $45,000

1836, 1838, AND 1839 GOBRECHT DOLLARS

The Silver Dollars produced by Christian Gobrecht between 1836 and 1839 are among the most beautiful American coins ever produced.

For many years, the Gobrecht Dollars were considered to be Patterns, but the large number of circulated 1836 and 1839 Silver Dollars, plus some deeper research into the Mint Archives, prove that some of these two dates were, indeed, intended for circulation. On the other hand, all 1838 Gobrecht dollars are unquestionably Patterns.

Gobrecht Dollars are found in an interesting variety of configurations. The obverses of the 1836 Gobrecht Dollars can be found with his name in the field below the base or on the base (it was moved there after Gobrecht was criticized for featuring his name so prominently). A little known fact is that the word LIBERTY is raised on the shield on the 1836-dated coins, but is incuse or recessed on those dated 1838 and 1839. The "skies" on the reverses of the 1836 Gobrecht Dollars are either empty or filled with 26 stars. Edges come plain or reeded. Although 600 Gobrecht silver dollars were struck in 1837, they bore the date 1836. Accordingly, there is no such thing as an 1837-dated dollar. Stars were added to the obverses of the 1838 and 1839 Silver Dollars; Gobrecht's name was deleted; the edges are found either plain or reeded; and the reverses are either plain or starred.

A confusing array of Restrikes was made in later years, beginning in the spring of 1859, according to recently discovered information. Planchet weights vary as do the alignment of the obverse and reverse dies relative to each other. Even today, experts are trying to develop better ways of classifying these rare and interesting coins.

1839 GOBRECHT DOLLAR

The Gobrecht Dollars were the first Silver Dollars produced at the Mint since 1804 (when some were struck from earlier-dated dies; also, we're not counting the 1804-dated Silver Dollars that were made specially in 1834 for diplomatic presentation purposes). While the design eventually transformed into the Seated Liberty Silver Dollar in 1840, the Gobrecht Dollars continue to command the respect and admiration of collectors.

Designed by Christian Gobrecht. The obverse shows Miss Liberty in a flowing gown sitting on a rock. Her left hand holds a staff surmounted by a Liberty Cap; her right hand steadies a shield and holds a band bearing the word LIBERTY. The date appears at the base of the obverse, below the rock. Depending on the year and variety, the designer's name will either be missing from the coin, below the base of the rock, or on the base of the rock. The reverse features an eagle in flight heading towards the left side of the coin. Surrounding the eagle are the legends UNITED STATES OF AMERICA and ONE DOLLAR. Depending on the year and variety, the fields surrounding the eagle will be either plain or filled with 26 stars Standards: weight ranges from 412 to 417 grains, depending on the variety; composition ranges from .892 to .900 silver, the balance in copper, depending on the year and variety; diameter 38 mm. Edge: plain or reeded, depending on the year and the variety.

Rarity: Very Rare to Extremely Rare. Surprisingly, Gem Proofs of any date are Extremely Rare, whether as an Original or a Restrike.

Historical Value (1836 Dollar)		
Choice Proof		
1960: $1,750 •	1980: $5,500 •	2003: $15,000

Historical Value (1838 Dollar)		
Choice Proof		
1960: $2,500 •	1980: $7,500 •	2003: $40,000

Historical Value (1839 Dollar)		
Choice Proof		
1960: $2,500 •	1980: $7,500 •	2003: $40,000

The Act of April 2, 1792, which established the Mint, called for various denominations, including several in gold. However, it was not until 1795 that the first American gold coins were made. It is believed that George Washington wanted gold coins struck before his presidential term ended (he had been in office since 1789, accepted a second term in 1793, but had no desire for a third term). It is said that in October of 1795, Director of the Mint Henry DeSaussure delivered 100 Ten Dollar "Eagles" to Washington, who at the time lived in Philadelphia as it was the seat of the federal government. The coins had been designed by Robert Scot, and similar to the Half Eagles, featured a capped bust portrait of Liberty facing right. A Roman onyx cameo may have inspired the design. The reverse, an eagle with a wreath in its beak and palm branches grasped by its talons, may also have been inspired by early Roman art. The majority of 1795 Ten Dollar Gold Eagles have palm wreaths with 13 leaves. A very few examples are known with only nine leaves. Today, the "Nine Leaves" variety is considered a major rarity. The variety was not recognized until the last few decades, and less than 20 can now be traced. The Harry Bass Collection, on display at the museum of the American Numismatic Association, contains the finest known Mint State example. At least one or two repaired coins are also known. The 1795 Ten Dollar gold coins are an historic link to the early formation of the United States. President George Washington took a personal interest in the striking of these coins, per tradition. The 1795 Ten Dollar Eagle is a very scarce and popular first year of issue. The so-called "Small Eagle" design was produced for only three years. The "Nine Leaves" variety can only be described as the best of the best.

The 1795 "Nine Leaves" Ten Dollar is considered a major variety for the series. Many lesser known varieties exist of the 1795-1804 Ten Dollar gold coins, but are unrecognized in the standard catalogs. An excellent study of the subject has recently been published by Anton's of Portage, Michigan entitled *United States Ten Dollar Gold Eagles 1795-1804* by Anthony J. Taraszka.

Designed by Robert Scot. The obverse features a capped bust of Liberty facing right surrounded by 13 stars. The reverse displays an heraldic eagle clutching arrows and olive branches. Mintage for the issue is unknown. Standards: weight 17.50 grams; composition .916 gold/.083 silver and copper; diameter 33 mm. Edge: reeded.

Rarity: Less than 20 examples of the 1795 "Nine Leaves" Ten Dollar are known. Four or five Mint State coins are known. The finest coin certified is Choice Uncirculated MS-63.

1795 "NINE LEAVES" TEN DOLLAR GOLD

Photography courtesy Tom Mulvaney

Historical Value		
About Uncirculated		
1960: $1,000	1980: $12,500	2003: $75,000

The 1796 Quarter Dollar possesses the attributes required of a great coin: the mintage is tiny, it's a one-year type coin, plus it's the first year of issue for both the design AND the denomination.

The rarity of the 1796 Bust Quarter Dollar is partly a function of priorities, partly a function of demand, and partly a function of what metal was available. A look at the various denominations issued in 1796 indicates that most of the Mint's energies were focused on Large Cents. Silver Dollars were next, followed by the new Dime, then the Half Dime, the $5 Gold piece, and finally, the Quarter Dollar and other denominations. Apparently, there was little demand for a Quarter Dollar in 1796, quite possibly because none had ever been minted before, and depositors of silver bullion did not think to request them!

Many of the 1796 Quarter Dollars were preserved in high grade. Allegedly, Col. E.H.R. Green (son of Hetty Green, the "Witch of Wall Street") owned a hoard of over 200 Uncirculated 1796 Quarter Dollars, many of which were Proof-like. Supposedly, this hoard was distributed in the 1940s, but either the grades were overstated or they remain hidden, as nowhere near that number of high grade 1796 Quarter Dollars exists today. Another possibility is that they have become so widespread that they no longer enter the market with frequency.

Some 1796 Quarter Dollars exhibit what appear to be deep scratches at the edges or on the high points. These so-called "adjustment marks" were caused when overweight planchets were literally filed down to remove some of the excess silver. In many cases, the cuts from the file were so deep that they remained even after the coin was struck. Adjustment marks were a part of the normal process of making coins in the late 1700s and should not be confused with scratches and marks that occurred after the coins were struck.

1796 QUARTER DOLLAR

Most 1796 Quarter Dollars show weakness on the eagle's head. Because this high point on the reverse is opposite a high point on the obverse, the pressures used to strike the 1796 Quarter Dollars were incapable of forcing the metal into the deepest recesses of the die, except in rare instances.

Some of the Proof-like 1796 Quarter Dollars have been called "Proofs" or "Presentation Strikes" in the past. These exceptional coins were early strikes from fresh dies, minus any adjustment marks on the planchets, and they were struck sharply enough that the details on the eagle's head are full and complete. While no records confirm these special strikings, it is quite possible that they were made for presentation purposes to commemorate the beginning of the new denomination.

Deceptive counterfeits exist, primarily of low-grade examples. Because of the high value of any 1796 Quarter Dollar, the authors recommend authentication or certification of any contemplated purchase. In fact, it is a good rule of thumb to have any high value federal coin certified by one of the leading grading services.

Designed by Robert Scot. The obverse features a draped bust of Liberty with some of her hair tied back in a bow. LIBERTY appears above, the date below, and 15 stars are divided up on the sides (eight on the left, seven on the right). The reverse features a plain eagle with outstretched wings within a wreath of palm and olive branches. The outer legend reads UNITED STATES OF AMERICA. No denomination appears anywhere on the coin. Standards: weight 104 grains; composition .890 silver/.110 copper; diameter 27.5 mm. Edge: reeded.

Rarity: 6,146 struck. While most 1796 Quarter Dollars are well circulated, a surprisingly large number of Mint State pieces exist, including several Gems and even a Superb piece (or two).

Photography courtesy Tom Mulvaney

Historical Value		
Extremely Fine		
1960: $1,250	1980: $7,500	2003: $17,500

The 1796 Half Dollars are among the most rare and most desirable of all United States coins. Their minuscule mintage reflects the scarcity of silver in the earliest days of the Mint, plus the lack of requests for half dollars by bullion depositors. Likely, most who wanted large coins wanted Dollars as they were easier to count and keep track of. Those desiring coins for change and small transactions opted for Half Dimes and Dimes. Quarter Dollars and Half Dollars were in sort of a Never Never Land—in between the two limits of popularity!

Mint records indicate that no Half Dollars were delivered in 1796. Numismatic historians speculate that Half Dollars may have been struck in 1796, but not delivered by the coiner until early 1797, when 934 Half Dollars were recorded. The coins in the later delivery of Half Dollars in May of 1797 are all believed to be 1797 dated coins. Of the 934 1796 Half Dollars, very few have survived and most are in low grades. However, several high-grade 1796 Half Dollars exist, including some that have Proof-like surfaces.

The earliest 1796 Half Dollars show 15 stars on the front of the coin, representing each of the states then in the Union. Later versions show 16 stars, reflecting the expected admission of Tennessee as a state in 1797. The practice of adding a new star for each new state ended quickly as the engravers simply ran out of room for all of the stars! Soon thereafter, government officials decided to revert back to 13 stars, representing the original 13 colonies. Thus, all Half Dollars from 1801 have only 13 stars on the front.

Of the two 1796 Half Dollar varieties, the 16 Stars is the rarest. However, despite the difference in rarity, the frequency with which the two varieties have appeared at auction (at least over the last five years) is virtually identical.

Considerable demand exists for the 1796 and 1797 Half Dollars because they are the only dates of the Draped Bust/Plain Eagle design. Anyone working on a type set of eighteenth-century American coins must eventually face the challenges of locating and affording either of these important dates.

Designed by Robert Scot. The obverse features a draped bust of Liberty with some of her hair tied back in a bow. LIBERTY appears above, the date below, and stars are divided up on the sides (one variety has 15 stars, the other has 16 stars). The reverse shows a plain eagle standing on clouds with outstretched wings within a wreath of palm and olive branches. The outer legend reads UNITED STATES OF AMERICA. The denomination appears as the fraction "1/2" beneath the bow of the wreath. Standards: weight 208 grains; composition .892 silver/.108 copper; diameter 32.5 mm. Edge: lettered FIFTY CENTS OR HALF A DOLLAR.

Rarity: The mintage of 1796 Half Dollars is unknown but estimated to be under 1,000 based on the Mint's 1797 delivery figures. The total mintage of all 1796 and 1797 amounted to only 3,918 coins! Most 1796 Half Dollars are in poor condition, but a few remarkably nice examples exist, including some choice Uncirculated pieces. Of the 15 Star variety, the finest is an MS-64. The best of the 16 Star variety is an amazing MS-66!

Historical Value (15 Stars)		
Extremely Fine		
1960: $2,000 •	1980: $15,000 •	2003: $45,000

Historical Value (16 Stars)		
Extremely Fine		
1960: $2,000 •	1980: $16,500 •	2003: $50,000

Photography courtesy Tom Mulvaney

1854 AND 1855 PROOF "TYPE TWO" GOLD DOLLARS

The "Type One" Gold Dollar, released in 1849, was successful in commerce (mainly because Silver Dollars were not available in circulation after 1850), and many were struck. However, they were found to be inconvenient in size. At a tiny 12.7 millimeters in diameter, it was easily lost and too small to handle. Moreover, the small and simple design was susceptible to counterfeiting. In 1852, United States Mint officials began to experiment with annular (ring-form) Gold Dollars, thus enlarging the coin to a more manageable size.

No change occurred until James Ross Snowden took the place of R.M. Patterson as Mint Director. Snowden was then free to change Patterson's Gold Dollar. Physically, the new coin was wider and thinner, and intended to make the coin more convenient. However, the "Type Two" was a failure due to its design. The relief on the obverse was much too high, making it extremely difficult to strike with detail on Liberty's hair. The reverse was poorly executed because the inscription THE UNITED STATES OF AMERICA was directly opposite the wreath. The thinner planchet also aggravated the overall predicament.

The "Type Two" Gold Dollar lasted only three years: 1854 to 1856 (with those of 1856 being struck only in San Francisco). During two of those three years, Proofs of this design were minted at the Philadelphia Mint, in 1854 and 1855, although very few still exist. It is believed that only 11 to 12 "Type Two" Gold Dollars survived in Proof format, with the 1854 appearing rarer. In 1997, an 1854 realized a stunning $193,600 at auction, while an 1855 realized an equally impressive $121,000 in the same sale. The Proof "Type Two" Gold Dollar is considered one of the most desirable gold Type coins in the U.S. series.

Type coins are ones that are collected by the Type without regard to date or mint mark. Many collectors try to obtain one of each Type for different series. Mint State examples of the "Type Two" Gold Dollar are quite scarce, Proof examples are coins most collectors only dream of.

Designed by James B. Longacre. The obverse features a bust of LIBERTY wearing a feather headdress. The words UNITED STATES OF AMERICA are found at the periphery. The reverse shows the words 1 DOLLAR, and a wreath encircles the date. Standards: weight 1.672 grams; composition .900 gold/.100 copper; diameter 15 mm. Edge: finely reeded.

Rarity: Four examples of the 1854 Proof are known, including an impaired example in the Smithsonian Institution. It is estimated that seven-to-eight Proof 1855's still survive.

1855 PROOF "TYPE TWO" GOLD DOLLAR

Photography courtesy David Akers & Tom Mulvaney

Historical Value (1854)		
Choice Proof		
1960: $3,500	1980: $35,000	2003: $150,000

Historical Value (1855)		
Choice Proof		
1960: $3,500	1980: $35,000	2003: $125,000

In 1870, a new United States Mint opened at Carson City, Nevada. Because of the Comstock Lode and other mineral discoveries, the West was producing an abundance of precious metals. It was felt that a coining facility in Carson City, only about 15 miles from the Comstock Lode, would be useful to the inhabitants of the territory. On March 10, 1870, the first Carson City Double Eagles were delivered by the coiner. A total of only 3,789 were struck for the year. Most were used for commercial purposes in Nevada and the surrounding territory. The key word is used, for the average 1870-CC Double Eagle is well worn and seldom seen above Very Fine condition. Nearly every coin is also heavily abraded with signs of extensive circulation.

The 1870-CC Double Eagle is highly sought after for several key reasons. First, Carson City coinage is very popular. Many individuals collect only coinage from that Mint. There is a great interest in the early West and relics from that part of American history. Collecting United States Double Eagles is also very popular. They are the largest and most substantial regular issue United States gold coin. With the exception of the 1870-CC, a complete set of Carson City Double Eagles can be completed relatively easy. The 1870, however, is a real "stopper." The demand far exceeds the supplies of the "King of Carson City Gold". It is by far the best known and most highly sought after gold coin from the Carson City Mint.

Nearly all examples of this great rarity are owned by serious collectors and are seldom offered for sale. The demand for scarce date Double Eagles is at an all-time high, prompted in part by the availability of 1856-S and, in particular, 1857-S coins from the *SS Central America* hoard brought to market in 2000-2002. New price records are broken nearly every time a nice 1870-CC appears at auction.

While most examples of the 1870-CC Double Eagle are genuine, fakes are known to exist. Unscrupulous individuals could very easily add the tiny "CC" mint marks to the far more common 1870 Double Eagle. As with most great coins, authentication is an important issue.

Designed by James B. Longacre. The obverse features the portrait of Miss Liberty facing left, wearing a coronet, and surrounded by 13 stars. The reverse features an outspread eagle and shield design. Mintage for this issue is 3,789 coins. Standards: weight 33.436 grams; composition .900 gold/.100 copper; diameter 34 mm; net weight .96750 oz pure gold. Edge: reeded.

Rarity: Most experts agree that between 35-50 examples are known to exist in all grades. Most are very well worn, with extensive bag marks. Just a few are known in relatively high-grade condition, and they command a solid six-figure price when they appear on the market. The finest known examples are About Uncirculated.

1870-CC DOUBLE EAGLE

Historical Value (1854)		
Extremely Fine		
1960: $2,500	1980: $25,000	2003: $125,000

On September 12, 1857, the steamship *SS Central America* sank in the Atlantic Ocean, 200 miles off the coast of North Carolina, on the way to New York with treasure fresh from the California Gold Rush. On board was an incredible quantity of gold bars, gold dust, and over 7,000 gold coins. Unfortunately, nearly 600 people were also making the trip home from the land of opportunity. When the ship sank below the waves, 425 lives were lost. The story of the *SS Central America* is one the most heart wrenching episodes of bravery and courage in American history. Because of a Herculean effort on the part of the passengers and crew, 153 passengers survived the ravages of the storm.

The ship and her golden bounty lay on the ocean floor in 7,200 feet of water for the next 130 years. In 1985, a group of explorers and investors formed the Columbus-America Discovery Group to locate the treasure. The wreck was found in September 1986. It was one the largest discoveries of treasure ever found. Over the next few years, the artifacts were brought to the surface. A legal battle ensued with insurance companies over the ownership of the find. A settlement was reached, and the gold was finally brought to market. The California Gold Marketing Group, headed by Dwight Manley, was formed to market the rare coins and gold bars.

Nearly all of the 1857-S Double Eagles from the *SS Central America* are pristine in appearance, and some very choice examples of a few earlier issues, notably 1856-S, were found as well. Prior to the find, early Double Eagles from the 1850s were nearly impossible to locate in higher states of preservation. Now, for a relatively small investment, one can own a tangible piece of this incredibly important chapter of American history.

1857-S DOUBLE EAGLE

It has been reported that the movie rights to the fascinating book *Ship of Gold in the Deep Blue Sea* have been purchased by a major movie studio. The story of the *SS Central America* is captivating, and the 1857-S Double Eagles may one day appear on the silver screen.

Designed by James B. Longacre. The obverse features the portrait of Miss Liberty facing left, wearing a coronet, and surrounded by 13 stars. The reverse features an outspread eagle and shield design. Mintage for this issue is 970,500 coins. Standards: weight 33.436 grams; composition .900 gold/.100 copper; diameter 34 mm; net weight .96750 oz pure gold. Edge: reeded.

Rarity: Prior to the discovery of the *SS Central America* hoard, the 1857-S Double Eagle was moderately scarce, but virtually unknown in choice condition. The *SS Central America* hoard contained over 5,000 examples of the 1857-S, many of which are incredible, radiant Gems. The fabulous preservation of these treasure coins is what makes this issue truly great. No other coins from this period can be found in nearly the same condition as the day they left the Mint.

Photography courtesy New York Mint & Tom Mulvaney

Historical Value		
Choice Uncirculated		
1960: $250	1980: $3,500	2003: $8,500

1794 "STARRED REVERSE" LARGE CENT

One of the more curious American coins (and a classic rarity) is the 1794 "Starred Reverse" Cent, technically known as Sheldon-48, from Dr. William H. Sheldon's *Penny Whimsy*, a book describing all of the Large Cents varieties from 1793 to 1814. A close look at the back of this fascinating coin reveals tiny stars hidden in the tooth-like border decorations.

Apparently, the engraver of the "Starred Reverse" Cent started the die for the back of the coin by stamping a ring of 94 stars near the outer edge. Such a border is unheard of on any United States coin issued for circulation, but a precedent exists in the Pattern Quarter Dollar of 1792 (also a Top 100 coin), which shows a border of 87 tiny stars. In fact, it was once believed that the die for the "Starred Reverse" Cent was a leftover die from the 1792 Pattern Quarter, until someone actually counted the stars!

Raised borders are placed on coins to aid in their stacking and to prevent wear to the field or lower surface of the coin. Without borders, the high points of coins rock against each other, resulting in a precarious stack that falls over easily. A look at the very first U.S. Large Cents shows the evolution of the borders from a plain, raised lip on the 1793 Chain Cents, to a raised ring of beads on the 1793 Wreath Cents, to the heavy denticles on the 1794 Cents--all the result of the search for a "perfect" raised border.

Perhaps because the ring of stars was considered unsatisfactory as a border, the engraver completed the die by adding denticles (the tooth-like projections pointing in from the outer edge), some of which hid or obliterated the underlying stars. Most of the surviving examples of the 1794 "Starred Reverse" Cent show much wear and/or corrosion, but a collector only needs to see a single star to make a positive attribution of this rarity. As one might expect, the more stars that are visible, the more valuable the coin.

The 1794 "Starred Reverse" Large Cent is a great coin but was undiscovered or unappreciated for over 85 years. The legendary dealer Henry Chapman is credited with the discovery of this important variety in the 1870s. The discovered coin was sold by the Chapman bothers in an 1880 auction for the modest sum of $4.25.

Designed by Robert Scot. The obverse features a bust of Liberty facing right, her hair flowing loosely behind her head. A Liberty Cap and supporting pole appear behind her head. LIBERTY appears above the bust, the date below. The reverse shows the words ONE CENT within a plain wreath, the fraction "1/100" below, and UNITED STATES OF AMERICA surrounding. Standards: weight 208 grains; composition pure copper; diameter 28 mm. Edge: lettered "ONE HUNDRED FOR A DOLLAR."

Rarity: Rare. Today, less than 100 "Starred Reverse" Cents are known. None have been found better than Extremely Fine.

1794 "STARRED REVERSE" LARGE CENT

Historical Value
Very Fine
1960: $1,500 • 1980: $10,000 • 2003: $75,000

Today, the 1864 Proof "Small Motto" Two Cent piece is represented by a mere handful of pieces and ranks as one of the rarest major varieties in all of American numismatics. Two significant varieties are recognized of the 1864 Two Cent piece: the Small Motto and Large Motto variants. The size difference refers to the motto "IN GOD WE TRUST." The difference is subtle, but easily recognized when the two varieties are compared side-by-side. Collectors soon discovered that the Small Motto variety was considerably rarer than the Large Motto Variety.

The Two Cent piece was an odd, short-lived denomination. The United States Two Cents is an unusual denomination that first appeared during a period of coin shortages caused by the Civil War. Attempts to introduce the Two Cents denomination occurred in 1806 and 1836, but both efforts failed due to technical considerations. In 1863, Mint officials revived the idea of a Two Cents Coin simultaneous with their plans to reduce the weight and metal content of the bulky, Copper-Nickel Indian Head Cent. The new coin featured a patriotic design (a Union Shield) and the first instance of the religious motto "IN GOD WE TRUST" on a circulating coin.

In anticipation of an eager demand and wide circulation for the new coin, the Mint struck nearly 20 million 1864 Two Cent pieces, mostly of the Large Motto variety, plus several hundred Proofs, of which only a few were of the Small Motto variety. In later years of the series, the number of coins struck for circulation decreased while the number of Proof coins struck for collectors increased. By 1865, approximately 14 million Two Cent pieces were struck; by 1866, only three million were struck; and by 1872, the last year circulating pieces were made, only 65,000 were struck. For example, in the final year (1873), no Two Cent pieces were struck for circulation at all and only Proof examples were made! Mike Kliman's 1977 book *The Two-Cent Piece and Varieties* remains a standard reference guide for these coins.

Designed by James Barton Longacre. The obverse shows a Union shield with a pair of crossed arrows behind. The motto IN GOD WE TRUST appears on a scroll above the shield; strands of leaves are draped on either side of the shield. The date appears at the bottom of the obverse. The reverse shows the denomination "2 CENTS" within a wreath, all surrounded by the legend UNITED STATES OF AMERICA. Standards: weight 96 grains; composition .950 copper/.050 tin and zinc; diameter 23 mm. Edge: plain.

Rarity: Extremely Rare.

1864 PROOF "SMALL MOTTO" TWO CENT PIECE

Historical Value		
Choice Proof		
1960: $1,500	1980: $5,000	2003: $35,000

1867 PROOF "WITH RAYS" SHIELD NICKEL

The 1867 Proof "With Rays" Shield Nickel is a mysterious, major rarity. Per one account, A. Louden Snowden, Chief Coiner at the time, refused to strike any Proofs of the 1867 "With Rays" Nickels, citing difficulties caused by the presence of the rays. However, the existence of some three-to-four dozen specimens indicates that somebody decided to strike them.

The "Nickel" (as we now know our Five Cent pieces) was a new invention in 1866. From 1794 to the early 1860s, the silver Half Dimes served admirably as our Five Cent denomination, but in 1862 the uncertain outcome of the Civil War caused hoarding of anything of value, including the silver coins then in circulation. To make up for the shortage of Half Dimes, the Treasury issued small 5 Cent notes called Fractional Currency. Fractional Currency circulated widely and was produced in such quantities that the Treasury was unable to redeem them all with gold and silver. Thus, the Nickel was born; its primary purpose was to replace the 5 Cent Fractional Currency notes.

"Nickel" is a misnomer, for the main metal in a Five Cent piece is copper, with nickel making up only 25% of the alloy. Nor were Nickels meant to replace the Half Dime. In fact, Nickels and Half Dimes were both minted simultaneously until 1873 when the Half Dime was finally phased out.

The first Nickels had an alternating series of 13 stars and 13 rays surrounding the numeral "5" on the back of the coin. Because the copper and nickel alloy was so hard, the Mint had problems with dies cracking and breaking prematurely. In early 1867, the decision was made to remove the rays from the reverse to improve the life of the dies. Yet, in spite of this change, most Shield Nickels continued to show cracks and breaks.

The exact mintage of the 1867 Proof "With Rays" Nickels is unknown and unrecorded. *A Guidebook of United States Coins* lists a mintage of 25+. The experts at the Professional Coin Grading Service list a mintage of 35 pieces in their Population Report, yet they report having certified 38 examples. Assuming that some of these may represent re-submissions of the same coin, one must still factor in the coins graded by other certification services, leading to the conclusion that as many as 40 to 50 examples may exist. Examination of the coins themselves indicates that at least two varieties exist. One variety could be Proofs that were actually struck in 1867; Proofs of the other variety may have been re-struck in later years.

While we may never know the exact mintage for this important coin, a significant rarity it remains, earning it a place in America's Top 100 coins.

Designed by James Barton Longacre. The obverse shows a Union shield with a pair of crossed arrows behind and near the base of the shield, somewhat similar to that used on the 1864 Two Cent piece. The motto IN GOD WE TRUST appears in an arc above the shield, and the date appears at the bottom of the obverse. The reverse shows a large "5" within a circle of stars and rays. The legend UNITED STATES OF AMERICA appears in an arc above the circle and the word "CENTS" appears beneath. Standards: weight 5 grams; composition .750 copper/.250 nickel; diameter 21 mm. Edge: plain.

Rarity: Extremely Rare. A few Gem Proofs represent the finest examples of this rare Nickel.

1867 PROOF "WITH RAYS" SHIELD NICKEL

Historical Value		
Choice Proof		
1960: $1,500	1980: $5,000	2003: $45,000

Mint reports indicate that 4,000 1827 Quarter Dollars were struck, but this number appears to be erroneous, as no examples struck for circulation have ever been found. Joseph J. Mickley received four Proofs in change from the Mint in 1827, and for several decades, these were the only ones known to exist. Now, however, there are believed to be as many as 10 Proof examples.

Because of this date's rarity, Restrikes were made in later years (1858-1859) using a different reverse. Restrikes have been found made of copper, on regular silver planchets, and even struck over an 1806 Quarter Dollar! In 1860, to prevent further Restrikes, Mint Director James Ross Snowden seized all old dies and placed them in his personal vault.

The difference between Originals and Restrikes is easy to determine. Originals used a reverse die of 1828 with a curled base on the 2 of the denomination, while Restrikes used a reverse die of 1819 with a flat base on the 2 of the denomination. Also, Restrikes are usually found with heavy die rust (now in the form of raised pimples) on both sides.

The Original 1827 Quarter Dollar has always been recognized as a classic rarity. Early collector demand is probably the reason restrikes were produced in the 1850s. The Original 1827 Quarter Dollar is usually only available when great collections are sold.

Designed by John Reich. The obverse features a draped bust of Liberty facing left, wearing a freedman's cap banded with the word LIBERTY. 13 stars appear near the edge (seven on the left side, six on the right). The date appears below the bust. The reverse features an eagle with outstretched wings and a shield on its chest. In its talons, the eagle holds an olive branch and a bunch of arrows. A scroll with E PLURIBUS UNUM hovers above the eagle's head. The outer legend reads UNITED STATES OF AMERICA and the denomination "25 C." appears beneath the eagle. Standards: weight 104 grains; composition .890 silver/.110 copper; diameter 29 mm. Edge: reeded.

Rarity: Extremely Rare, approximately 10 Originals known, all struck as Proofs. The finest known Original is a Gem Proof-66.

1827 "ORIGINAL" QUARTER DOLLAR

Photography courtesy Tom Mulvaney

Historical Value		
Choice Proof		
1960: $7,000	1980: $40,000	2003: $100,000

1801, 1802 AND 1803 PROOF SILVER DOLLARS

The Proof Silver Dollars of 1801, 1802, and 1803 are all extremely rare, valuable, and desirable, although none of them were made anywhere near the dates on the coins, nor do they share any die characteristics with any real Silver Dollars made from 1801-1803. On the other hand, they share a close kinship with the 1804 Silver Dollar (the #1 coin in the Top 100 list).

Exactly when the 1801-1803 Proof Bust Dollars were made is unclear. It may have been around 1834 when the first 1804 Silver Dollars were made. Or they may have been created (or the dies finished) around 1858. The weights of the coins may help to place or confirm the striking date; at around 420 grains each, they are closer to the Trade Dollars (minted from 1873 to 1885) than either Bust Dollars or Seated Liberty Dollars.

The 1801-1803 Proof Bust Dollars all feature unusual characteristics:

1) they share a reverse die with the "Original" (Class I) 1804 Silver Dollars.

2) the edge border on both sides is beaded, an invention credited to William Kneass in 1828.

3) the edge lettering appears to have been added to the coins after they were struck.

Today, the 1801-1803 Proof Silver Dollars rarely appear on the market. In fact, in recent years, four 1804 Silver Dollars have appeared at auction compared to no Proof 1801's, two Proof 1802's, and only two Proof 1803's during the same time period!

Today, Bust Dollars are among the most popular United States coin series. Several collectors have made serious attempts to assemble sets of the series by date and die variety. Bust Dollars remain a tangible link to the early commerce of the United States. Because of their considerable size, Bust Dollars are one of the most physically impressive coins and are always in demand.

Designed by Robert Scot. The obverse features a draped bust of Liberty with some of her hair tied back in a bow. LIBERTY appears above, the date below, and 13 stars are divided up on the sides (seven on the left, six on the right). The reverse features an heraldic eagle with outstretched wings (similar to the one on the Great Seal of the United States). In its beak, the eagle holds a scroll with the words E PLURIBUS UNUM. In its left talon, the eagle grasps an olive branch; in its right talon, it holds a bunch of arrows. Clouds and 13 stars appear above the eagle. The outer legend reads UNITED STATES OF AMERICA. No denomination appears anywhere on the coin. Standards: weight, around 420 grains; composition .900 silver/.100 copper; diameter 39-40 mm. Edge: lettered HUNDRED CENTS ONE DOLLAR OR UNIT.

Rarity: Extremely Rare. Exact mintages are unknown but cannot be more than a few of each date. Most of the 1801-1803 Proof Silver Dollars have survived in excellent condition. Those that have appeared on the market in recent years have all graded Proof-64 or better.

Photography courtesy Doug Plasencia at Bowers and Merena Galleries

Historical Value (1801, 1802, 1803)		
Choice Proof		
1960: $4,500	1980: $35,000	2003: $150,000

1851 SILVER DOLLAR

Experts recognize two varieties of the 1851 Silver Dollar: Originals made in 1851 for circulation and Proof Restrikes made several years later. Only 1,300 Original 1851 Silver Dollars were made for circulation. Price guides show a complete range of valuations from Very Good to Uncirculated, but mid-range grades are extremely rare. A collector is more likely to find a Mint State 1851 Silver Dollar than one in Fine condition. A true circulation strike 1851 Silver Dollar is an underrated rarity. Proof Restrikes are relatively "common" by comparison, with a surviving population estimated to number in the range of 20-30 pieces.

Designed by Christian Gobrecht. The obverse shows Miss Liberty in a flowing gown sitting on a rock. Her left hand holds a staff surmounted by a Liberty Cap; her right hand steadies a shield and holds a band bearing the word LIBERTY. 13 stars appear in an arc around Miss Liberty and the date appears at the base of the obverse, below the rock. The reverse shows an eagle with a shield on its chest, an olive branch in its right talon, and a bunch of arrows in its left. The words UNITED STATES OF AMERICA appear above the eagle; the abbreviation ONE DOL. appears below. Standards: weight 26.7 grams; composition .900 silver/.100 copper; diameter 38 mm. Edge: reeded.

Rarity: Very Rare. Only 1,300 examples were struck for circulation, plus an estimated 50 Proofs. The best Original circulation strikes cluster around the MS-64 grade, with perhaps one or two Gems known to exist (in 1997, an MS-65 example realized $57,500). Since 1995, only two Proof Original 1851 Silver Dollars have appeared at auction, both selling for less than $20,000. Proof Restrike 1851 Silver Dollars appear at auction at the rate of about one-to-two pieces per year, so collectors have plenty of opportunities to purchase one of these rarities, as long as they can finance them. The high-water mark for an 1851 Proof Restrike Silver Dollar since 1995 is $37,375 for a Gem Proof-65.

Historical Value		
Choice Proof		
1960: $1,500 •	1980: $7,500 •	2003: $37,500

Photography courtesy David Akers & Tom Mulvaney

1852 SILVER DOLLAR

The story of the 1852 Silver Dollar parallels that of the 1851 Silver Dollar (also a Top 100 coin). Both dates are found as 1) Originals struck for circulation, 2) Originals struck as Proofs, and 3) Proof Restrikes made years later.

At a mintage of 1,100 pieces, the 1852 is slightly rarer than the 1851, but the grades of the known examples are distributed more evenly across the grading scale, all the way from Good to full Mint State. Proof Originals are exceedingly rare: only one 1852 Proof Original Silver Dollar has appeared at auction, where a Proof-60 example sold for $17,600 in 1998. Proof Restrikes of the 1852 Silver Dollar are known in both silver and copper. The 1852 Proof Restrike appears at auction almost as often as the 1851 Proof Restrike Silver Dollar, but usually brings a slightly higher price because of its slightly higher rarity.

Designed by Christian Gobrecht. The obverse shows Miss Liberty in a flowing gown sitting on a rock. Her left hand holds a staff surmounted by a Liberty Cap; her right hand steadies a shield and holds a band bearing the word LIBERTY. 13 stars appear in an arc around Miss Liberty and the date appears at the base of the obverse, below the rock. The back shows an eagle with a shield on its chest, an olive branch in its right talon, and a bunch of arrows in its left. The words UNITED STATES OF AMERICA appear above the eagle; the abbreviation ONE DOL. appears below. Standards: weight 26.7 grams; composition .900 silver/.100 copper; diameter 38 mm. Edge: reeded.

Rarity: Very Rare. Only 1,100 examples were struck for circulation, plus an estimated 35 Proofs. Original examples are very rare in any condition, but become extremely rare in Mint State. Original Proofs are exceedingly rare. Proof Restrike 1852 Silver Dollars are very rare, but can usually be found in high grades, including Choice to Gem Proof.

Photography courtesy The Stellar Collection & Tom Mulvaney

Historical Value (1801, 1802, 1803)		
Choice Proof		
1960: $1,500 •	1980: $7,500 •	2003: $35,000

1893-S MORGAN DOLLAR

The 1893-S Silver Dollar has the lowest mintage of any of the Morgan Dollars issued between 1878 and 1921, making it one of the rarest and most valuable coins in the series. In fact, the 1893-S Silver Dollar is the most valuable of any of the dates made for circulation. The only other date that is more valuable is the 1895, a date that is believed to have been issued only as a Proof. The Morgan Dollar, because of its large size and silver content, is perhaps the most popular series of American coins ever produced. Because so many people are familiar with the rarity of the 1893-S Silver Dollar and because so many people still need the coin to complete their set, the authors feel it deserves a place in the pantheon of the Top 100 American coins.

Designed by George Morgan. The obverse features a large head of Miss Liberty facing left, wearing a freedman's cap banded with the word LIBERTY and a wreath of American agricultural produce. E PLURIBUS UNUM appears in an arc around Liberty's head; the date appears below. 13 stars are divided on either side of the obverse (seven on the left and six on the right). The reverse features a plain eagle with wings raised and outstretched, holding an olive branch and arrows in its talons. IN GOD WE TRUST appears above the eagle in script. A wreath arcs around below the eagle and the legends UNITED STATES OF AMERICA and ONE DOLLAR appear in a circular arrangement on the outside of the coin. The mint mark can be seen just below the bow of the wreath on the reverse. Standards: weight 26.7 grams; composition .900 silver/.100 copper; diameter 38 mm. Edge: reeded.

Rarity: Rare. Only 100,000 1893-S Silver Dollars were struck for circulation. Uncirculated examples are very rare, although a handful of Gems are known and at least two Superb pieces have appeared on the market. In November of 2001, a Superb Gem 1893-S Silver Dollar sold for $414,000 at auction.

Historical Value
Choice Uncirculated
1960: $2,500 • 1980: $35,000 • 2003: $125,000

Photography courtesy The Stellar Collection & Tom Mulvaney

1870-S SILVER DOLLAR

Mint records contain no evidence that any 1870-S Silver Dollars were struck, yet around a dozen examples are known to exist. Each year, the Philadelphia Mint prepared dies for the branch mints. Unfortunately, no records survive of shipments of Silver Dollar dies to San Francisco in 1869 or 1870. However, Coiner J.B. Harmstead returned two dies without mint marks in May 1870, anticipating the proper replacements from the Philadelphia Mint. The 1870-S Silver Dollars were all struck from the same pair of dies, but the mint mark is different from that on any S-Mint Half Dollars of the period. Harmstead may have received some 1870 dated obverse dies. However, without any mint marked reverses, he may have added his own, thus accounting for the difference in the appearance of the mint mark on the 1870-S Silver Dollars.

Designed by Christian Gobrecht. The obverse shows Miss Liberty in a flowing gown sitting on a rock. Her left hand holds a staff surmounted by a Liberty Cap; her right hand steadies a shield and holds a band bearing the word LIBERTY. 13 stars appear in an arc around Miss Liberty, and the date appears at the base of the obverse, below the rock. The back shows an eagle with a shield on its chest, an olive branch in its right talon, and a bunch of arrows in its left. The words UNITED STATES OF AMERICA appear above the eagle; the abbreviation ONE DOL. appears below. A scroll with the motto IN GOD WE TRUST hovers above the eagle. The mint mark appears just below the eagle. Standards: weight 26.7 grams; composition .900 silver/.100 copper; diameter 38 mm. Edge: reeded.

Rarity: Extremely Rare. The estimated population for this date is a mere 12 coins. Most are well circulated and/or accompanied by a problem of one sort or another (test cut, corrosion, cleaning, repaired initials). The finest example appears to be the Proof-like About Uncirculated example from the Norweb Collection.

Photography courtesy The Stellar Collection & Tom Mulvaney

Historical Value
Extremely Fine
1960: $15,000 • 1980: $75,000 • 2003: $200,000

1804 "13 STARS" QUARTER EAGLE

In 1804, the Philadelphia Mint struck two varieties of the Quarter Eagle: one with 14 stars on the reverse and a second with 13 stars. One of the most intriguing aspects of the "13 Stars" Quarter Eagle is its connection to the Ten Cent denomination. In the early nineteenth century, the U.S. Mint made every effort to conserve steel for dies. Thus, many dies were overpunched from one year to another.

In the case of early Quarter Eagles and Dimes, the two denominations were approximately the same size and had an identical reverse motif, so the Mint conveniently used one reverse die for both denominations. The reverse die found on the 1804 "13 Stars" Quarter Eagle, interestingly, was first used on the 1802 Quarter Eagle. The Mint saved it until 1804, when it was put into action to strike Dimes. It was used yet again to strike the 1804 "13 Stars" Quarter Eagle. Such a cross-denomination link is extremely rare in American numismatics, but does occur with a few other Dimes and Quarter Eagles.

Only seven 1804 "13 Stars" Quarter Eagles are known. The most recent appearance was in October 2001, when a solid AU specimen appeared as part of the Dallas Bank Collection sold by Sotheby's and Stack's. John Jay Pittman also owned an example of this rare variety; his coin was sold in 1998 by David W. Akers.

Designed by Robert Scot. The obverse features a woman wearing a Liberty cap surrounded by stars. The word LIBERTY is featured at the top with the date located at the bottom. The reverse features an eagle surrounded by the words UNITED STATES OF AMERICA. Above the eagle's head is a field of stars and six clouds. Standards: weight: 4.37 grams; composition .916 gold/.083 copper; diameter 20 mm. Edge: reeded.

Rarity: About seven examples are currently known.

Photography courtesy David Akers & Tom Mulvaney

Historical Value		
Extremely Fine		
1960: $2,500 •	1980: $7,500 •	2003: $75,000

1841 QUARTER EAGLE

Like many of the coins described in this book, the 1841 Quarter Eagle has an uncertain history. One bizarre aspect of the coin is that it was struck in Proof format. The U.S. Mint did not begin to sell Proofs to the public until 1859, and prior to that, Proofs were only struck for special circumstances. Another curiosity is that no Quarter Eagle circulation strikes were produced in 1841 per Mint records (however, these are not always complete). Furthermore, the Philadelphia Mint struck Quarter Eagles for circulation every year from 1834 to 1862 except for 1841.

Why the coin was struck remains uncertain. There may have been no demand for Quarter Eagles that year, and therefore the Mint only struck about 20-25 Proofs. One numismatist speculated that a group of foreign dignitaries visited Philadelphia in 1841 and the Quarter Eagles were presented as gifts. However, the fact that nearly every 1841 Quarter Eagle was discovered in the United States refutes that theory. Regardless of how they came into existence, the 1841 Quarter Eagles have had a storied past in numismatic circles. For many years, it was assumed that only a handful of specimens were known. In fact, one example sold privately for $3,000 in 1930. As more coins surfaced, the coin's value decreased sharply, with one specimen selling for $605 at auction in 1940. Today, it is believed that 15-18 are known. The finest known example, graded Proof 64, was last sold by Bowers and Merena Galleries as part of the Harry W. Bass, Jr. collection.

Designed by Christian Gobrecht. The obverse features a figure of Liberty wearing a coronet. The word LIBERTY is inscribed on the headband. 13 stars encircle the portrait with the date at the bottom. The reverse features a spread eagle located in the center with the words UNITED STATES OF AMERICA written at the edge. The denomination 2½ D. is featured at 6:00. Standards: weight 4.18 grams; composition .900 gold/.100 copper; diameter 18 mm. Edge: reeded.

Rarity: Between 15-18 specimens are known.

Photography courtesy David Akers & Tom Mulvaney

Historical Value		
Extremely Fine		
1960: $3,500 •	1980: $20,000 •	2003: $75,000

1854-S QUARTER EAGLE

The 1854-S Quarter Eagle has largely been forgotten by most numismatists, despite its incredibly low mintage of 246 and that only a dozen survivors are known. As recently as 1982, a specimen changed hands for under $10,000, representing an astounding value considering its overall rarity. As one researcher stated back in 1952, the 1854-S Quarter Eagle is "one of the most underrated United States coins in any metal…and [is] completely free of the stigma of Mint experimentation and chicanery." However, with a recent auction appearance over $100,000, it appears that gold specialists have indeed "re-discovered" the 1854-S Quarter Eagle.

Exactly why only 246 Quarter Eagles were minted in 1854 remains uncertain. Purportedly, the Mint could not obtain the necessary acids to remove silver from the impure California gold. But the San Francisco Mint was able to strike an ample supply of Eagles and Quarter Eagles. The true reason was that depositors of gold requested higher and lower denominations, and the $2.50 and $5 were in between, and thus few were made.

Interestingly, not a single 1854-S Quarter Eagle was known until 1910, when Edgar Adams reported that he discovered a specimen. Since then, numerous other examples have surfaced, though the total population known does not exceed 10. Most pieces are heavily worn; the AU-50 Bass coin ranks as the finest known.

Designed by Christian Gobrecht. The obverse depicts a figure of Liberty wearing a coronet. The word LIBERTY is inscribed on the headband. 13 stars encircle the portrait with the date at the bottom. The reverse features a spread eagle located in the center with the words UNITED STATES OF AMERICA written at the edge. The denomination 21/2 D. is featured at 6:00. Standards: weight 4.18 grams; composition: .900 gold/.100 copper; diameter 18 mm. Edge: reeded.

Rarity: Approximately 10 coins are known, all of which are worn to varying degrees.

Historical Value
Very Fine
1960: $1,500 • 1980: $15,000 • 2003: $75,000

Photography courtesy Numismatic Guaranty Corporation

1863 PROOF QUARTER EAGLE

The story of the 1863 Quarter Eagle begins with its total mintage of only 30 Proof examples.

Of the original 30 that were struck, no more than 15 left the portals of the Mint. Demand for Proof gold was lukewarm at the time, so the Mint melted Proofs year after year. The 1863 Quarter Eagles were were among those melted. Harold P. Newlin, a famous researcher in his day, corresponded with legendary collector T. Harrison Garrett about the 1863 Quarter Eagle. In a letter dated September 13, 1883, Newlin writes: "I have recently secured two pieces which were obtained at the mint in the year they were struck, by the gentleman from whom I got them. They are the gold dollar and quarter eagle of 1863. They are in beautiful proof condition. The former is rare and the latter in my estimation is the rarest of the series of quarter eagles."

Although more specimens surfaced after 1883, the gist of Newlin's message still holds true: the 1863 Quarter is one of the rarest, if not THE rarest of the Quarter Eagles.

Designed by Christian Gobrecht. The obverse features a figure of Liberty wearing a coronet. The word LIBERTY is inscribed on the headband. 13 stars encircle the portrait with the date at the bottom. The reverse shows a spread eagle located in the center with the words UNITED STATES OF AMERICA written at the edge. The denomination 21/2 D. is featured at 6:00. Standards: weight 4.18 grams; composition .900 gold/.100 copper; diameter 18 mm. Edge: reeded.

Rarity: Approximately 12 coins are known today.

Historical Value
Choice Proof
1960: $1,500 • 1980: $15,000 • 2003: $40,000

Photography courtesy Heritage Numismatic Auctions, Inc.

1797 "16 STARS REVERSE" HERALDIC HALF EAGLE

Whereas there are perhaps 50 to 100 1797 Half Eagles featuring 16 obverse stars, only one coin, the "16 Stars Reverse," is known with the Heraldic "Large" Eagle on the reverse, as opposed to the more typical small eagle.

When the Half Eagle first debuted in 1795, the coin featured a "small eagle" reverse designed by Robert Scot. However, the public criticized the Half Eagle's reverse, stating that the eagle appeared scrawny and weak. In response to the public disapproval, Scot revamped the Half Eagle reverse design and introduced the Heraldic Eagle reverse.

This unique coin is permanently housed in the Smithsonian Institution, having been donated by the executors of the estate of Eli K. Lilly.

Designed by Robert Scot. The obverse depicts Liberty wearing a soft liberty cap and facing right. The stars are placed around the edge of the obverse, and the date is located at the base. The Heraldic Eagle reverse features an outstretched eagle that wears a 13-stripe shield. The wings are partially covered by a flowing scroll inscribed E PLURIBUS UNUM. Clouds are placed above the eagle's head. Standards: weight 8.75 grams; composition .9167 gold/.0833 copper; diameter 25 mm. Edge: reeded.

Rarity: Unique. Since the only known specimen has not traded hands in recent decades—and may not ever again—it is difficult to assign a value to the coin. However, it is comparable in rarity to the 1870-S Three Dollar piece and 1822 Half Eagle, both of which are valued in excess of $1,000,000.

Historical Value
Extremely Fine
1960: $2,500 • 1980: $50,000 • 2003: $300,000

Photography courtesy Smithsonian Institution and Douglas Mudd

1819 HALF EAGLE

The Philadelphia Mint frequently reused coinage dies. The 1819 "5D over 50" Half Eagle exemplifies this, as a blundered die from 1818 was used again in 1819, despite its erroneous denomination marking. Apparently, an engraver carelessly punched "50" into the original die, but he eventually realized his mistake. He then punched the correct "5D" over the first impression, although rather obvious signs of the blunder still remained. The die was finally retired in late 1819 only because it had become worn.

It is also worth mentioning that official Mint records report that 51,723 Half Eagles were struck in 1819. Considering how scarce 1819 Half Eagles are, this is difficult to believe. Once again, 1818 obverse dies were probably used until they were worn beyond potential use. This policy of reusing dies year after year led to inaccurate and misleading mintage information, which has occasionally confused researchers. In any event, it is believed that around two dozen 1819 Half Eagles are known among all three varieties, although the 5D over 50 variety is the most famous.

Specimens regularly sell in the mid five-figure range. Even well-worn examples have no difficulty exceeding the $10,000 mark.

Designed by John Reich. The obverse features a large portrait of Liberty surrounded by 13 stars with the date below. The reverse shows an eagle shown with spread wings, holding an olive branch and arrows. Surrounding the eagle are the inscriptions UNITED STATES OF AMERICA and 5 D., with the motto E PLURIBUS UNUM above the eagle's head. Standards: weight 8.75 grams; composition .916 gold/.083 silver; diameter 25 mm. Edge: reeded.

Rarity: Between 20-24 1819 Half Eagles can be traced. However, 10 or so are of the 5D/50 variety.

Photography courtesy Tom Mulvaney

Historical Value (Half Eagle)			Historical Value (5D Over 50 Half Eagle)		
About Uncirculated			About Uncirculated		
1960: $1,500 • 1980: $25,000 • 2003: $45,000			1960: $1,500 • 1980: $25,000 • 2003: $35,000		

1825/4 HALF EAGLE

1825/4 HALF
EAGLE

At the first United States Mint in Philadelphia (1792-1832), reusing dies over several years was not uncommon. The Mint operated on a tight budget, so it was necessary to recycle dies for as long as possible. In the case of the 1825/4 Half Eagle, a leftover 1824 die was repunched, thus changing the date from 1824 to 1825. However, the underlying digit "4" was still quite obvious, hence the moniker "1825/4 Half Eagle."

As a variety, the 1825/4 is one of the rarest of all United States gold coins. A surprise hit the numismatic world in 1978 when a long-lost 1825/4 Half Eagle reappeared on the market. That year, RARCOA auctioned the Nathan M. Kaufman collection, a group of coins that went untouched for decades. Unfortunately, the coins had been displayed in a bank conference room in Marquette, Michigan, in a most unsafe manner; they were tacked to the wall, creating unsightly rim bumps, on some (but not all) specimens. Luckily, Kaufman's 1825/4 Five escaped unscathed and fetched a strong $140,000 in the sale.

Designed by John Reich. The obverse depicts a large portrait of Liberty surrounded by 13 stars with the date below. The reverse features an eagle with spread wings, holding an olive branch and arrows. Surrounding the eagle are the inscriptions UNITED STATES OF AMERICA and 5 D., with the motto E PLURIBUS UNUM above the eagle's head. Standards: weight 8.75 grams; composition .916 gold/.083   silver; diameter 25 mm. Edge: reeded.

Rarity: Two coins are known: an Uncirculated (or possibly Proof) specimen and an AU-50. The Eliasberg coin, the finer of the two, brought $220,000 in 1982.

Photography courtesy Tom Mulvaney

Historical Value
About Uncirculated
1960: $2,500 • 1980: $125,000 • 2003: $250,000

1832 "12 STARS" HALF EAGLE

1832
"12 STARS"
HALF EAGLE

The early Half Eagle series is filled with important rarities, of which the 1832 "12 Stars" Half Eagle is certainly a member. The 1832 "12 Stars" Half Eagle has only six specimens known in all grades, making it as rare or rarer, than each of the two varieties of the 1829 Half Eagle and the rare 1815. However, because an 1832 Half Eagle can be easily acquired with 13 stars, collectors often overlook these scarcer varieties.

In the past 10 years, two 1832 "12 Stars" Half Eagles have sold at auction. The first coin, an attractive Uncirculated specimen, sold for just under $300,000 in 1996. By comparison, an EF-45 sold for $159,000 just two years later. The Harry Bass Research Foundation also owns one specimen, which is currently on display at the museum of the American Numismatic Association in Colorado Springs, Colorado.

Designed by John Reich with modifications from William Kneass. The obverse features a large portrait of Liberty surrounded by 12 stars with the date below. The reverse shows an eagle with spread wings, holding an olive branch and arrows. Surrounding the eagle are the inscriptions UNITED STATES OF AMERICA and 5 D., with the motto E PLURIBUS UNUM above the eagle's head. Standards: weight 8.75 grams; composition .916 gold/.083 silver; diameter 22.5 m. Edge: reeded.

Rarity: Researchers estimate that six coins are known in all.

Photography courtesy Tom Mulvaney

Historical Value
Extremely Fine
1960: $3,500 • 1980: $45,000 • 2003: $125,000

1875 HALF EAGLE

The 1875 Half Eagle is one of the few coins that is more readily available in Proof than as a circulation strike. Only 220 Half Eagles were struck in 1875, including 200 coins made for general circulation. Many of the Philadelphia Half Eagles of this era are quite scarce. The 1875 Half Eagle, however, is considered one of the greatest rarities of the United States gold series. With only 200 coins minted, it is understandable that just a few survived the melting pots. Apparently, none were saved for numismatic purposes. Very few other Liberty gold coins are seen as seldom as the 1875 Half Eagle. Collectors are usually able to acquire an example of this fabled rarity only when great collections cross the auction block. Proof examples are seen occasionally. Probably half of the original mintage of 20 still is in existence.

Designed by Christian Gobrecht. The obverse portrays Liberty with a coronet facing left and surrounded by 13 stars. The reverse features an eagle with spread wings clutching arrows and olive branches. Mintage for circulation strikes is 200 coins, 20 for Proofs. Standards: weight 8.359 grams; composition .900 gold/.100 copper; diameter 21.6 mm; net weight .24287 oz pure gold. Edge: reeded.

Rarity: Less than eight circulation strike examples are known, none of which are Mint State. The finest known specimen is About Uncirculated. There are probably 8-10 Proof coins that still survive.

Historical Value
About Uncirculated
1960: $750 • 1980: $25,000 • 2003: $75,000

Photography courtesy Doug Plasencia at Bowers and Merena Galleries

1798/7 TEN DOLLAR GOLD (TWO VARIETIES)

Because early United States gold coins became worth more for their bullion than for their face value, most of these issues were destroyed. Only 135,592 Ten Dollar gold coins were struck from 1795-1804. From 1797-1804, the Heraldic Eagle design was produced. The great rarities of this design are two varieties dated 1798/7. On one variety, there are nine stars on the left and four on the right of the obverse. The other variety has seven stars on the right and six stars on the left. Records indicate that on February 17, 1797, 900 Ten Dollar Eagles were delivered from the Mint. It is thought that these were the 9 X 4 variety. On February 28, only 842 of the 7 X 6 variety were delivered, these figures being the estimates of Walter Breen based upon his interpretation of Mint records. Both of these historic coins are rare, but the 1798/7 seven stars left, six stars right, is one of the major rarities of the era. Less than 20 examples are known in all grades of this variety. Most examples of both varieties are well-worn or damaged though a few Mint State examples do exist. The early Ten Dollar gold coins from 1795-1804 are rare, but completing a set is possible. There are no "stoppers" like the Early Half Eagle, which has several issues of which only a few are known. For this reason, Ten Dollar gold coins from 1795-1804 are very popular coins.

Designed by Robert Scot. The obverse features a capped Liberty facing right surrounded by 13 stars. The reverse displays an heraldic eagle clutching arrows and olive branches. Mintage for the issue is 900 of the 9 X 4 variety and 842 of the 7 X 6 variety. Standards: weight 17.50 grams; composition .9167 gold/.0833 silver and copper; diameter 33 mm. Edge: reeded.

Rarity: The 1798/7 9 X 4 stars is rare, and fewer than 100 are known in all grades. Several Mint State examples remain. The 1798/7 7 X 6 stars is extremely rare and seldom encountered. It is estimated that less than 20 examples exist, with a couple of Mint State examples at the high end of the condition scale.

Photography courtesy Tom Mulvaney

Historical Value (7x6 Stars)	Historical Value (9 x 4 Stars)
About Uncirculated	About Uncirculated
1960: $2,500 • 1980: $25,000 • 2003: $95,000	1960: $1,000 • 1980: $12,500 • 2003: $35,000

1808 QUARTER EAGLE

A popular method of collecting U.S. coins is to buy one coin of each design type, one of each date or mint variety. The 1808 Quarter Eagle has the distinction of being a one-year type. As such, it is a coin sought by both type collectors and Quarter Eagle specialists. It is also an extremely scarce coin, with approximately 50-60 pieces known in total. Of those, many are well worn with only a few high-grade specimens in existence.

The finest known 1808 Quarter Eagle, generally considered an MS-64, was sold in the mid-1980s for a figure close to $100,000. It was once part of the collection built by former Congressman Jimmy Hayes of Louisiana.

Designed by John Reich. The obverse features a woman wearing a Phrygian liberty cap. 13 stars are present at the obverse periphery. The date is located below the truncation of the portrait. The reverse portrays a spread eagle displayed at the center with the motto E PLURIBUS UNUM inscribed above the eagle's head. The words UNITED STATES OF AMERICA are written at the circumference with the denomination 2½ D. at 9:00. Standards: weight 4.37 grams; composition .916 gold/.083 copper; diameter 20 mm. Edge: reeded.

Rarity: Between 50-60 specimens are known from an original mintage of 2,710.

Photography courtesy Tom Mulvaney

Historical Value
About Uncirculated
1960: $2,000 • 1980: $17,500 • 2003: $35,000

1875 TEN DOLLAR GOLD

The 1875 Ten Dollar has the grand distinction of possessing the lowest mintage figure of any United States gold coin. Only 100 examples were struck for circulation, with 20 additional Proofs produced. This date ranks as one of the all time rarities of the Liberty Head series. Most coins struck during this time were melted, so very few circulation strike examples of the 1875 Eagle remain, and most are well worn. About Uncirculated is the finest known for the issue, with no Mint State specimens having ever been reported. This is one of the few United States rarities seen in Proof more frequently than in the circulation strike format. This probably depresses the price of the circulation strikes, for without the Proofs to meet the demands of date collectors, this issue would be much more expensive. The 1875 Ten Dollar Liberty is considered a landmark rarity and one of the most important coins of the United States gold series.

Designed by Christian Gobrecht. The obverse features a portrait of Liberty facing left surrounded by 13 stars. The reverse depicts an eagle with wings spread, clutching arrows and olive branches. Mintage for this issue is 100 circulation strikes and 20 proofs. Standards: weight 16.718 grams; composition .900 gold/.100 copper; diameter 27 mm; net weight .48375 oz pure gold. Edge: reeded.

Rarity: This date is extremely rare with seven-to-eight circulation strikes currently known. Probably an equal number of Proofs remain. The finest surviving circulation strike is About Uncirculated. Several Choice Proofs survive.

Photography courtesy Tom Mulvaney

Historical Value
About Uncirculated
1960: $750   •   1980: $20,000   •   2003: $80,000

The 1854-O Double Eagle is one of the great rarities of the Liberty Head series. The date boasts a tiny mintage of just 3,250 pieces. Most of the Double Eagles were immediately placed into circulation, as today there are no known Mint State examples. The average coin is moderately worn, with scattered bag marks. Many have been harshly cleaned in the past. Genuine examples of this date exhibit raised die lines on the TY of LIBERTY. A few examples are also seen with minor die defects.

Designed by James B. Longacre. The obverse features a portrait of Miss Liberty facing left, wearing a coronet, surrounded by 13 stars. The reverse features an outspread eagle and shield design. Mintage for this issue is 3,250 coins. Standards: weight 33.436 grams; composition .900 gold/.100 copper; diameter 34 mm; net weight .96750 oz pure gold. Edge: reeded.

Rarity: In 1854 3,250 Double Eagles were minted in New Orleans. We estimate that only 20-30 examples are known in all grades, and there are no known Mint State coins reported.

1854-O DOUBLE EAGLE

Photography courtesy Jeff Garrett & Tom Mulvaney

Historical Value		
Extremely Fine		
1960: $500	1980: $35,000	2003: $75,000

1856-O DOUBLE EAGLE

Southern gold coinage has been very popular with collectors for many years. One of the "crown jewels" of the market is the 1856-O Double Eagle. But just 2,250 examples were struck for the year in New Orleans. Only one set of dies is thought to have been used for the production of 1856-O Double Eagles. The coins were circulated extensively, as most of the survivors are well worn. Many of the higher grade examples exhibit partially Proof-like surfaces. The finest known example is fully Proof-like, and considered by many experts to be a Proof or presentation piece. It is one of the most spectacular rarities in the United States gold series. This date is the rarest New Orleans Double Eagle and is one of the rarest non-Proof coins of the series.

Designed by James B. Longacre. The obverse features a portrait of Miss Liberty wearing a coronet, facing left, surrounded by 13 stars. The reverse features an outspread eagle and shield design. Mintage for this issue is 2,250 coins. Standards: weight 33.436 grams; composition .900 gold/.100 copper; diameter 34 mm; net weight .96750 oz pure gold. Edge: reeded.

Rarity: With a tiny mintage of only 2,250 coins, this date is very rare by any standard. Only 15-20 are known today in all grades. The lone Mint State example known is a Choice Proof-like example and is considered by many to be a presentation strike.

Photography courtesy David Akers & Tom Mulvaney

Historical Value		
Extremely Fine		
1960: $500	1980: $35,000	2003: $85,000

In 1860, Anthony Paquet, an engraver at the Philadelphia Mint, modified the reverse design for the Double Eagle. The new design is very similar to the standard issue, but the reverse letters are much taller and slender in appearance. There are also several technical variations with regard to the positioning and size of the lettering. In late 1860, the Paquet reverse became the standard design that was adopted for the regular issue coinage of 1861 Double Eagles. Dies were shipped to the branch Mints of New Orleans and San Francisco. Actual coinage on high-speed presses began in January 1861 in Philadelphia, but Mint Director James Ross Snowden felt that the die would be unsuitable for high-speed production. Snowden recalled the new design and ordered the Philadelphia Mint issue to be melted. The entire Philadelphia run was destroyed, with the exception of a few coins. Snowden also ordered production to cease in New Orleans and San Francisco. The order reached New Orleans in time to prevent any coinage. Because the transcontinental railroad was still several years away from completion, and the telegraph did not extend past St. Joseph, Missouri, the directive to stop coinage did not reach San Francisco until 19,250 coins had been struck, but no effort was made to recall the issue.

Designed by James B. Longacre. The obverse features a portrait of Miss Liberty wearing a coronet, facing left, surrounded by 13 stars. The reverse features an outspread eagle and shield design. Mintage for this issue is 19,250 coins. Standards: weight 33.436 grams; composition .900 gold, .100 copper; diameter 34 mm; net weight .96750 oz pure gold. Edge: reeded.

Rarity: Today there are probably 200-300 examples known in all grades of the 1861-S Paquet Reverse Double Eagle. Most are well worn and very baggy in appearance. It is obvious that the entire mintage was placed into extensive circulation. There are no Mint State examples known.

Photography courtesy David Akers & Tom Mulvaney

Historical Value
About Uncirculated
1960: $1,500 • 1980: $7,500 • 2003: $35,000

1879 "Schoolgirl" Silver Dollar Pattern

George T. Morgan experimented with different designs, including several Pattern coins in 1879. The Schoolgirl Pattern obverse features the head of a young-looking girl, her hair combed back and falling about her shoulders. The reverse features a defiant eagle perched atop a standard with the words "In God We Trust," a motif he had used earlier on an 1877 Pattern Half Dollar.

1879 "Quintuple Stella" Pattern in Gold

The 1879 Patterns reflect the Mint's attention to two concepts: a metric coin and an international coin. Both concepts converged on the $4 and $20 Gold Patterns, known as "Stellas" and "Quintuple Stellas," respectively. The Quintuple Stella is almost identical in appearance to a regular 1879 Double Eagle, but the obverse stars were replaced with "*30*G*1.5*S*3.5*C*35*G*R*A*M*S*" There is no large star (Stella) on the back of the "Quintuple Stella," nor even the word "Stella," but because the two coins arose from the same idea and because the obverse legends are similar, the larger coin became known as the "Quintuple Stella."

1882 "Shield Earring" Silver Dollar Pattern

In 1882, George T. Morgan created just one Silver Dollar Pattern coin for a Silver Dollar: the famous "Shield Earring" Dollar, so-named because of the shield-shaped earrings worn by Miss Liberty. The reverse features a defiant eagle facing right, with an olive branch in one talon and a bunch of arrows in the other. "Shield Earring" Dollar Patterns are known in Silver and Copper, both of which are extremely rare.

Photography courtesy Rarities LLC and Tom Mulvaney

Historical Value (1879 Schoolgirl Stella)		Historical Value (1879 Quintuple Stella)	
Choice Proof		Choice Proof	
1960: $1,000 • 1980: $25,000 • 2003: $75,000		1960: $4,000 • 1980: $100,000 • 2003: $350,000	

Historical Value (Earring Dollar)
Choice Proof
1960: $1,000 • 1980: $25,000 • 2003: $75,000

About Uncirculated – a coin close to Uncirculated or Mint State condition, with slight traces of wear on the high points

Adjustment mark – file marks caused when metal was removed from the planchet to bring it down to the proper weight

Alloy – a blended mixture of two or more metals used to make a coin

Bi-Metallic – the use of two metals in an unmixed or unalloyed state

Bullion – any form of gold or silver traded for its metal value

Bullion dealer – a trader in bullion

Business strike – a coin made for circulation or use in general commerce

Bust – usually the portrait on a coin

Circulated – a coin that is worn from use in general commerce

Coin press – the machine used to stamp or strike a coin

Commemorative – a coin struck to honor a place, event, or person

Counterfeit – a fake or false coin

Denomination – the stated value on a coin

Denticles – the toothlike projections around the outer rim of a coin

Die – the cylindrical piece of steel used to stamp a coin

Double Eagle – an American $20 gold piece

Doubloon – a Spanish gold coin weighing approximately 420 grains (.875 Troy ounce)

Eagle – an American $10 gold piece

Electrotype – a counterfeit coin made by joining electroplate impressions from a real coin

Extremely Fine – a well-preserved coin with excellent details and a trace of original luster

Fusible Alloy – the 1792 One Cent pieces made of an alloy of copper and a small amount of silver

Gem – an exceptionally well-preserved coin

Good – a heavily worn coin that retains very little of the original details

Grain – a unit of measuring weight, 480 grains to the Troy ounce

Greenback – America's paper money, first introduced around the time of the Civil War

Guinea – British gold coins from the 1700s, slightly larger than an American Quarter Dollar

Half Eagle – an American $5 gold piece

Heraldic Eagle – an eagle with outstretched wings and a shield on its chest

Legend – the wording on a coin

Lettered Edge – the edge of a coin that has been impressed with words

Matte Proof – a Proof coin with a dull, sandblast finish

Mint – the official government buildings where coins are made

Mintage – the number of coins that were made

Mint State – a condition that is brand new or Uncirculated

Monetize – the official act of turning a coin into money

Numismatics – the study of coins

Numismatist – a collector and student of coins

Obverse – the front of a coin

Pattern – a coin made to test new designs for possible use on coins made for circulation

Pedigree – the chain of ownership of a particular coin

Planchet – the metal blank that eventually becomes a coin

Presentation strike – a coin made expressly for presentation to a VIP or government official

Proof – a specially prepared coin usually with reflective, mirror-like surfaces

Prooflike – an Uncirculated coin that looks like a Proof

Quarter Eagle – an American $2.50 gold coin

Rarity – a determination of how rare or common a particular coin is

Reeded – the ridges on the edge of a coin

Reverse – the back of a coin

Spanish Doubloon – a Spanish gold coin weighing approximately 420 grains (.875 Troy ounce)

Superb – a coin that is nearly perfect

Type Set – a collection of all the major design types in a denomination or series of coins

Uncirculated – a coin that has no wear or friction (synonymous with Mint State)

Undertype – traces of an original coin that remain after having been struck again by new dies

Variety – minor or major differences between coins of the same design

Very Good – a coin that is very worn but still legible

Bass, Harry W.

Harry Bass is regarded not only as a famous collector of United States gold coins, but also as a student of the series. After starting his collection in the 1960s, Bass acquired some of the greatest rarities in U.S. gold, including memorable items such as the 1870-S Three Dollar piece, an 1875 Three Dollar piece, many of the rare early Half Eagles, an 1854-S Quarter Eagle, and countless others. In a style similar to Virgil Brand, Bass did not mind buying multiples of major rarities. In addition, he collected U.S. gold by die combination—something that most numismatists largely ignore. Most of the Bass collection was sold in 1999 and 2000 by Bowers and Merena Galleries, with the balance of the holdings on display at the American Numismatic Association museum in Colorado Springs, CO.

Boyd, Frederick C.C.

Frederick Boyd was born in New York City in 1886 and began collecting coins at an early age. Although collecting eventually became his main numismatic focus, he dealt in coins for a brief period of time, as demonstrated by a small mail bid auction he held in 1913. His primary occupation was managing the Union News Company, which maintained newsstands at railroad stations across America. With his considerable income, Boyd acquired many premier rarities in the United States coinage series, including rarities such as the 1804 dollar and the 1854-S Half Eagle. When Boyd decided to sell his holdings in the 1940s, Numismatic Gallery of New York was chosen to be the auctioneer. So spectacular were Boyd's coins that the auctions were called "The World's Greatest Collection."

Brand, Virgil M.

The Brand collection ranks as one of the largest and most extensive coin collections—or hoards some would argue—ever assembled. Virgil M. Brand was born in 1861 in Blue Hill, Illinois. He eventually moved to Chicago, where he formed a highly successful brewing company. Brand began to collect coins in 1879, although he did not begin to record these acquisitions until 1889. Brand recorded each coin purchase in a large, leather-bound volume; these volumes are now in the American Numismatic Society library. Brand was one of the most active rare coin buyers in America, adding to his collection at an incredible rate without regard for duplication. For example, Brand owned six 1884 trade dollars—an amazing feat considering that only 10 were minted. Equally shocking, he owned five 1792 Silver Center cents, three Strawberry Leaf cents, four 1875 Three Dollar pieces, and 30 Stellas. When Brand died in 1926, his collection contained over 350,000 specimens. The Brand estate was so immense that it took over six decades to liquidate the collection. Brand's family began to sell the coins in the 1930s, and the last coins were sold by Bowers and Merena in 1984.

Browning, Jeff

The name Jeff Browning may be foreign to most numismatists, but his collection is now widely known. Browning was a major collector of United States gold coins, purchasing many important rarities in the 1960s and 1970s. Among his most important acquisitions was a complete set of United States Stellas, an 1804 "13 stars" Quarter Eagle, an 1870-CC double eagle, the 1861 Paquet double eagle, and a 1907 Ultra High Relief double eagle. He is also one of only a few numismatists to have ever owned a complete set of Liberty double eagles, including such rarities as the 1856-O, 1870-CC, and 1861 Paquet. His collection was sold in December 2001 as the Dallas Bank Collection in an auction conducted jointly by Sotheby's and Stack's.

Buss, Jerry

Although the coins are ranked #1, #2, and #6 in this book respectively, the 1804 Dollar, 1913 Nickel, and 1894-S Dime are often called "The Big Three" of American numismatics. Only a handful of collectors have ever owned this prestigious trio, of which Jerry Buss can be considered a member. A Los Angeles businessman, Buss is widely known for owning the Los Angeles Lakers basketball team. At one point, he also owned the Los Angeles Kings and the Great Western Forum. In the numismatic world, Buss acquired his three great rarities with the assistance of Superior Stamp and Coin in 1978 through 1979. The same firm later auctioned the coins in 1985.

The Carter Family

Amon Carter was a prominent Texas businessman whose activities included publishing the *Fort Worth Star-Telegram*, oil drilling, and co-founding American Airlines. The Carter collection contained many prominent United States rarities, including am 1822 Half Eagle, an 1875 Three Dollar piece, an 1815 Half Eagle, and an 1804 Dollar. After Amon Carter Sr. passed away, his son, Amon Carter, Jr. managed the collection. His holdings remained totally intact save for one coin: the 1822 Half Eagle. Josiah Lilly offered $60,000 for the coin, which the younger Carter felt was too tempting. After Amon Carter, Jr. died in 1982, the collection was sold at auction by Stack's in 1984.

Dunham, William F.

No discussion of important United States collections can exclude the William Forrester Dunham collection, sold in 1941. Dunham was born in Vermont in 1857, but later relocated to Chicago. He was a successful druggist and spent much of his earnings towards his fantastic collection. After his death in 1936, Dunham's collection was sold to B. Max Mehl, who, in turn, sold the collection via mail bid auction in 1941. Interest was so great that 2,500 catalogues were sold for $3 each. Although the collection contained many famous rarities, the 1804 Dollar and the 1822 Half Eagle were certainly the highlights. Interestingly, the 1804 Dollar realized $4,250, while the 1822 Half Eagle brought $11,575—a then-record amount for a U.S. coin.

Eliasberg, Louis E.

Louis Eliasberg is widely regarded as "The King of Coin Collectors," and for excellent reason. Although there have been many spectacular collections in the history of American numismatics, Eliasberg was the only individual to own every single major U.S. coin issue. In other words, he owned a complete United States coin collection. Born in 1896, Eliasberg later moved to Baltimore in 1907, where he established his highly successful banking business. Eliasberg was extremely fortunate in that many fabulous collections came on the market in the 1940s, the period in he was most active. In 1942, the New York firm of Stack's sold the John H. Clapp collection to Eliasberg in its entirety for $100,000. This transaction alone brought Eliasberg close to completion. After that monumental sale, Eliasberg picked the remaining rarities he needed from sales such as the F.C.C. Boyd collection. A few other coins were acquired via private treaty to complete the collection. Interestingly, it took no more than a decade to finish the collection, which remained intact until 1982. That year, Eliasberg's federal gold coins were sold at auction by Bowers and Merena, although the copper, nickel and silver specimens were not sold until 1996 and 1997. When the hammer fell on the last coin, the Eliabsberg collection grossed a record $45,000,000.

King Farouk of Egypt

The King Farouk collection was a result of the overindulgence and avarice that surrounded Farouk's reign in Egypt. Despite his seemingly unlimited budget, Farouk never seemed to have a true appreciation for United States coinage—he simply enjoyed buying whatever was available at virtually any price. Indeed, the key to success as a coin dealer in the 1940s was having King Farouk as a customer. Farouk was eventually exiled in the early 1950s, at which point Sotheby's was appointed to liquidate the king's substantial excesses. Unfortunately, many of the coins were lacquered before the auction, and the coins were grouped together sloppily in massive lots. The nearly priceless Judd 1776, for example, was grouped into a large lot of Patterns without description. The auction proved to be a field day for American collectors and dealers, who either attended in person or sent representatives to Egypt on their behalf. Many great collections, such as the Norweb and Pittman holdings, were formed with coins from the Farouk sale.

The Garrett Family

Regarded as one of the finest collections of coins ever assembled, the Garrett collection was completed by two generations during a span of over six decades. T. Harrison Garrett, the founder of the Baltimore and Ohio Railroad, started the collection in the late 1870s. However, he was killed in an untimely boating accident, which left the collection to his son, Robert Garrett. In 1919, the coins were once again transferred, this time to Robert's brother John Work Garrett, who proved to be more active in acquiring pieces for the collection. After Garrett's death in 1942, the holdings were bequeathed to Johns Hopkins University, which decided to liquidate the collection in the late 1970s. Bowers and Ruddy conducted four sales of the Garrett collection, which netted over $25,000,000 total.

Green, Colonel E.H.R.

Colonel E.H.R. Green was the son of Hetty Green, known to many as "The Witch of Wall Street." In 1917, the younger Green inherited massive amounts of money, which he spent on a wide variety of items, including rare coins. Like Virgil Brand, Green owned multiples of many major rarities. In fact, he owned all five 1913 Nickels known today! For comparison purposes, Green owned the entire sheet of "Inverted Jenny" stamps, which are regarded as the philatelic world's equivalent of the 1804 dollar. Green's massive collection was sold privately in the late 1930s and early 1940s, with the coins sold en bloc to major dealers. In order to buy one select rarity, dealers often were forced into buying entire sections of the collection.

Hydeman, Edwin

Some collections are known for being particularly extensive or all-encompassing, Edwin Hydeman chose to focus on major rarities. Among his most important holdings were an 1804 Dollar, a 1913 Nickel, and the unique 1866 "No Motto" Quarter and Half Dollar. Hydeman was the owner of a department store and sold his collection through Abe Kosoff in 1961. Although many of the coins met the reserves in the auction, some were retained and later sold by Kosoff later via private treaty. Interestingly, both the 1804 Dollar and 1913 Nickel landed in the Jerry Buss collection, a group of coins with a similar emphasis on major rarities.

Lilly, Josiah K.

Most numismatists forget about Josiah Lilly's world-class collection—until they walk into the Smithsonian Institute. Unbeknownst to most, one of the greatest collections still intact is that of Josiah K. Lilly, director of the pharmaceutical firm that bears his name. Not only is Lilly's name foreign to most numismatists today, but also he escaped notice during his heyday in the 1950s and 1960s. Most major collectors appeared at conventions, participated in public auctions, or were somehow known to the numismatic world. Lilly, on the other hand, operated in an extremely private manner, despite his substantial appetite and budget for rare gold coinage. Lilly died in 1966, at which point his collection was donated to the Smithsonian to offset an outstanding tax bill. Since then, the fabulous Lilly holdings have been placed on display, where they are admired by millions of visitors.

Mickley, Joseph J.

A true pioneer in U.S. numismatics, Joseph J. Mickley was one of the first major coin collectors in America. Born in 1799, Mickley began his pursuit of coins as a teenager, initially focusing on foreign coins from Europe. His tastes shifted later to American coinage, even though there were no coin dealers in the United States. Indeed, the first true full-time coin dealer was Ed Cogan, who did not open for business until 1858. As a result, Mickley's only viable trading partner was the United States Mint itself! Mickley was able to purchase many formidable rarities from the Philadelphia Mint, including a Class 1 1804 Dollar and many early proof sets. Mickley's collection was sold in 1867, where his prized 1804 Dollar realized $750. Although there were countless major rarities in the sale, American numismatics was still a young field at the time, and thus many scarce coins brought tiny premiums over face value.

Newcomer, Waldo

Waldo Newcomer, one of the lesser-known major collectors of the 20th century, owned many of the rarest coins in all of numismatics. A banker by profession, Newcomer called Baltimore, Maryland his home. Among the more important coins in his collection were an 1804 Dollar, a Brasher Doubloon, and an 1838-O Half Dollar. Newcomer elected to sell his collection gradually, beginning with a small auction in 1914, another in 1919, and several others into the 1920s and 1930s. Many coins from the Newcomer collection were later sold to the John Work Garrett, mostly through Wayte Raymond at the Scott Coin and Stamp Company.

The Norweb Family

The Norweb collection was assembled by a husband and wife team, although Mrs. Norweb was actually the more active participant. R. Henry Norweb, who owned mines in Canada, later became a U.S. ambassador. Interestingly, it was his wife, Emily, who took the most interest and negotiated many of the acquisitions. She had also inherited part of the collection. Among the notable rarities owned by the Norwebs included an 1827 Quarter, a Silver Center Cent, a 1792 Pattern Quarter, an 1815 Half Eagle, a fabulous Superb Gem 1861 Paquet Double Eagle, and many others. The Norwebs owned a Brasher Doubloon and a 1913 nickel at one point, but decided to donate the coins to the Smithsonian and the ANS, respectively. Bowers and Merena auctioned a portion of the Norweb collection in 1987 and 1988.

Parmelee, Lorin G.

The Lorin Parmelee collection is undeniably one of the finest assemblages of United States coins ever formed. Born in Vermont in 1827, Lorin Parmelee moved to Boston in 1849. He accumulated substantial wealth as a bean baker and supplied most restaurants in Boston with legumes. Parmelee became interested in coins by picking large cents out of circulation, which resulted in his special interest in copper coinage. His love of coins extended to all series, and hence he purchased almost every major rarity available to him. He also acquired several major collections intact, including the spectacular Bushnell collection of early American and colonial coinage. Parmelee's collection was auctioned in 1890, although many items were bought back and sold privately at a later date.

Pittman, John Jay

Not only was John Jay Pittman's collection one of the finest ever assembled, but also the story of how he formed the collection is truly fascinating. Unlike many of the collectors mentioned in this text, Pittman was not a particularly wealthy individual. He worked for Eastman Kodak in Rochester New York, where he held a respectable but not necessarily lucrative position in their chemical department. Rather than focus on major rarities, Pittman acquired coins that were esoteric, rare, and undervalued. Some of his favorite areas included scarce proof material and early American coinage. Pittman was also extremely careful in how and when he acquired coins for his collection. In 1946, for example, he decided not to participate extensively in the World's Greatest Collection auction, as he felt that he could acquire some of the coins later for substantially less at a later time. He was correct; many of the coins came on to the market two years later and could be had for a fraction of their original selling price. In another memorable event, Pittman mortgaged his house to attend the storied Farouk collection sale in Cairo. This spectacular 1954 auction contained many extreme rarities, such as the 1913 Nickel and the 1933 Double Eagle. Rather than compete on the premier rarities, Pittman was an aggressive bidder on the more esoteric items in the sale. Even though Pittman spent less than $100,000 on his entire collection, his holdings were sold for over $25,000,000 in 1997 and 1998. Many coins were originally purchased for $50-$100 in the 1940s, yet realized well in excess of $100,000 in the late 1990s. Pittman's collection was a testimony to the investment potential of United States coins.

Trompeter, Ed

Proof gold coins are regarded as the "crème de la crème" of American numismatics, as they tend to have miniscule original mintages and low survival rates. For many collectors, owning just one specimen is a true accomplishment. Yet, Ed Trompeter miraculously assembled a complete set of regular production proof gold, which would include coins minted from 1860-1915. He also acquired major rarities such as an 1855 Proof Gold Dollar, the 1872 Amazonian set, a complete set of Stellas, an 1874 Bickford Eagle, a Quintuple Stella, and a 1907 Ultra High Relief. A portion of his collection was auctioned in 1992, shortly before his death, but the balance of the collection did not appear on the market until 1998. In fact, Trompeter's Half Eagle, Eagles, Double Eagles, and the Amazonian set traded hands for a record $15,177,500 in the summer of 1998.

Wilkison, John

As a group, gold Patterns are among the rarest and most beautiful coins in American numismatics. In fact, a dozen of the coins listed in this book are technically gold Patterns (1849 $20, 1907 UHR $20, Judd-1776, Amazonian set, 1877 $50, 1907 UHR $10, Stellas, 1804 $10, 1907 RE $10, 1874 Bickford $10 and 1879 Quintuple Stella). These coins are also exceedingly scarce. As one can imagine, assembling a set of gold Patterns is a daunting task, but John Wilkison accomplished the extraordinary feat of owning nearly every known gold Pattern. His collection was sold intact in 1973 to Paramount International Coin Corporation, and subsequently, the set was traded in its entirety to A-Mark Financial. In the late 1970s, individual pieces were sold to various collectors and dealers, including notable rarities such as the Judd 1776 and the Amazonian set.

Woodin, William H.

William H. Woodin was born in Berwick, Pennsylvania on May 27, 1868. An eclectic personality, Woodin was involved in numerous activities, ranging from writing children's songs to serving as Secretary of the Treasury under Franklin D. Roosevelt. He was also extremely active in numismatics and assembled one of the greatest and most exotic collections of U.S. coins ever, including major rarities such as the unique 1870-S Three Dollar piece. One fascinating story involving Woodin is the history of the 1877 gold Half Unions. These fabulous coins, ranked #13 in this text, appeared on the private market briefly around 1909. Woodin acquired the two known specimens for $10,000 apiece—a record sum for the time. However, the United States government seized the coins, but compensated Woodin with an incredible assortment of rare and unique Pattern coinage. Many of the Patterns on the numismatic market today likely originated from the transaction. Woodin sold his collection at auction in 1911 through dealer Thomas L. Elder.

PRICE HISTORY 100 GREATEST

RANK	DESCRIPTION	GRADE	The Year 1960	The Year 1980	TODAY
1	1804 Bust Dollar	Choice Proof	$ 30,000.00	$ 250,000.00	$ 3,000,000.00
2	1913 Liberty Head Nickel	Choice Proof	$ 50,000.00	$ 250,000.00	$ 2,000,000.00
3	1933 Double Eagle	Choice Uncirculated	$ 25,000.00	$ 250,000.00	$ 7,500,000.00
4	1849 Double Eagle	Choice Proof	$ 100,000.00	$ 1,000,000.00	$ 7,500,000.00
5	1907 Ultra High Relief	Gem Proof	$ 20,000.00	$ 250,000.00	$ 1,000,000.00
6	1894-S Barber Dime	Choice Proof	$ 15,000.00	$ 100,000.00	$ 750,000.00
7	1907 Judd 1776	Gem Proof	$ 25,000.00	$ 500,000.00	$ 7,500,000.00
8	1943 Copper Cent	Extremely Fine	$ 5,000.00	$ 20,000.00	$ 50,000.00
9	1822 Half Eagle	Extremely Fine	$ 25,000.00	$ 650,000.00	$ 2,500,000.00
10	1885 Trade Dollar	Choice Proof	$ 15,000.00	$ 100,000.00	$ 1,000,000.00
11	1872 Amazonian Set	Choice Proof	$ 15,000.00	$ 500,000.00	$ 3,000,000.00
12	1776 Continental Dollar	Uncirculated	$ 300.00	$ 10,000.00	$ 35,000.00
13	1877 Half Union Fifty Dollar (Type One)	Choice Proof	$ 50,000.00	$ 1,000,000.00	$ 4,500,000.00
13	1877 Half Union Fifty Dollar (Type Two)	Choice Proof	$ 50,000.00	$ 1,000,000.00	$ 4,500,000.00
14	1909-S VDB Cent	Choice Uncirculated	$ 150.00	$ 750.00	$ 1,500.00
15	1793 Chain Cent	Extremely Fine	$ 750.00	$ 10,000.00	$ 25,000.00
16	1876-CC Twenty Cent	Choice Uncirculated	$ 7,500.00	$ 50,000.00	$ 100,000.00
17	1907 Ultra High Relief	Gem Proof	$ 20,000.00	$ 250,000.00	$ 2,500,000.00
18	1792 Half Disme	Very Fine	$ 500.00	$ 5,000.00	$ 35,000.00
19	1838-O Bust Half Dollar	Proof	$ 5,000.00	$ 75,000.00	$ 200,000.00
20	1794 Bust Dollar	Extremely Fine	$ 6,500.00	$ 25,000.00	$ 125,000.00
21	1870-S Half Dime (*Unknown Until 1978)	Choice Uncirculated		$ 425,000.00	$ 750,000.00
22	1854-S Half Eagle	About Uncirculated	$ 5,000.00	$ 200,000.00	$ 750,000.00
23	1856 Flying Eagle Cent	Choice Proof	$ 1,250.00	$ 3,500.00	$ 15,000.00
24	1873-CC "No Arrows" Seated Dime	Choice Uncirculated	$ 25,000.00	$ 250,000.00	$ 750,000.00
25	1907 High Relief	Choice Uncirculated	$ 500.00	$ 7,500.00	$ 15,000.00
26	1915-S Pan Pacific Fifty (Octagonal)	Choice Uncirculated	$ 2,500.00	$ 15,000.00	$ 35,000.00
26	1915-S Pan Pacific Fifty (Round)	Choice Uncirculated	$ 3,500.00	$ 20,000.00	$ 45,000.00
27	1875 Three Dollar	Choice Proof	$ 7,500.00	$ 75,000.00	$ 125,000.00
28	1879 Flowing Hair Stella	Choice Proof	$ 5,000.00	$ 25,000.00	$ 75,000.00
28	1879 Coiled Hair Stella	Choice Proof	$ 10,000.00	$ 75,000.00	$ 250,000.00
28	1880 Flowing Hair Stella	Choice Proof	$ 10,000.00	$ 45,000.00	$ 125,000.00
28	1880 Coiled Hair Stella	Choice Proof	$ 15,000.00	$ 100,000.00	$ 350,000.00
29	1792 Disme (Copper)	Extremely Fine	$ 1,000.00	$ 17,500.00	$ 75,000.00
30	1870-S Three Dollar	Very Fine	$ 25,000.00	$ 650,000.00	$ 2,500,000.00
31	1792 Silver-Center Cent	Very Fine	$ 1,500.00	$ 25,000.00	$ 85,000.00
32	1787 Fugio Cents	Uncirculated	$ 50.00	$ 500.00	$ 2,500.00
33	1861 "Paquet" Double Eagle	About Uncirculated	$ 5,000.00	$ 75,000.00	$ 350,000.00
34	1792 Birch Cent	Very Fine	$ 1,500.00	$ 35,000.00	$ 200,000.00
35	U.S. Assay Fifty Dollar Gold Coins	Extremely Fine	$ 1,500.00	$ 6,500.00	$ 15,000.00
36	1815 Half Eagle	Extremely Fine	$ 2,500.00	$ 45,000.00	$ 100,000.00
37	1793 Strawberry Leaf Cent	Fine	$ 2,500.00	$ 30,000.00	$ 200,000.00
38	1798 Half Eagle Small Eagle	Extremely Fine	$ 3,500.00	$ 75,000.00	$ 250,000.00
39	1844-O Half Eagle Proof	Choice Proof	$ 2,500.00	$ 75,000.00	$ 850,000.00
39	1844-O Eagle Proof	Choice Proof	$ 2,500.00	$ 75,000.00	$ 1,250,000.00
40	1884 Trade Dollar	Choice Proof	$ 7,500.00	$ 50,000.00	$ 200,000.00
41	1873-CC "No Arrows" Seated Quarter	Uncirculated	$ 3,500.00	$ 75,000.00	$ 175,000.00
42	1849-C "Open Wreath" Gold Dollar	Extremely Fine	$ 7,500.00	$ 75,000.00	$ 275,000.00
43	1838 Ten Dollar Proof	Choice Proof	$ 5,000.00	$ 100,000.00	$ 500,000.00
44	1804 Ten Dollar Plain 4	Proof	$ 3,500.00	$ 50,000.00	$ 150,000.00
45	1866 "No Motto" Seated Quarter	Choice Proof	$ 25,000.00	$ 75,000.00	$ 350,000.00
46	1866 "No Motto" Seated Half Dollar	Choice Proof	$ 20,000.00	$ 75,000.00	$ 350,000.00
47	1866 "No Motto" Seated Dollar Pattern	Choice Proof	$ 15,000.00	$ 100,000.00	$ 1,000,000.00
48	1833 Half Eagle Proof	Gem Proof	$ 3,500.00	$ 100,000.00	$ 500,000.00
49	1834-1838 Classic Half Eagles Type Proof	Choice Proof	$ 2,500.00	$ 25,000.00	$ 65,000.00
50	1927-D Double Eagle	Gem Uncirculated	$ 1,500.00	$ 150,000.00	$ 500,000.00
51	1829 Half Eagle (Large Planchet)	Uncirculated	$ 3,500.00	$ 50,000.00	$ 150,000.00
51	1829 Half Eagle (Small Planchet)	Uncirculated	$ 3,500.00	$ 45,000.00	$ 125,000.00
52	1907 "Rolled Edge" Ten Dollar	Choice Uncirculated	$ 3,500.00	$ 40,000.00	$ 85,000.00
53	1933 Ten Dollar	Choice Uncirculated	$ 2,500.00	$ 75,000.00	$ 150,000.00
54	1848 Quarter Eagle CAL	Uncirculated	$ 1,500.00	$ 20,000.00	$ 45,000.00

RANK	DESCRIPTION	GRADE	The Year 1960	The Year 1980	TODAY
55	1842 "Small Date" Seated Quarter	Choice Proof	$ 2,500.00	$ 15,000.00	$ 85,000.00
56	1792 Pattern Quarter (Copper)	Extremely Fine	$ 2,500.00	$ 30,000.00	$ 175,000.00
57	1817/4 Bust Half Dollar	Extremely Fine	$ 3,500.00	$ 40,000.00	$ 200,000.00
58	1853-O "No Arrows" Seated Half Dollar	Fine	$ 3,500.00	$ 25,000.00	$ 175,000.00
59	1916 Standing Quarter	Choice Uncirculated	$ 750.00	$ 2,500.00	$ 7,500.00
60	1851-O Seated Dollar (*Previously Unknown)	Choice Proof			$ 250,000.00
61	1802 Half Dime	Extremely Fine	$ 2,000.00	$ 25,000.00	$ 75,000.00
62	1796 "With Pole" Half Cents	Very Fine	$ 750.00	$ 7,500.00	$ 25,000.00
62	1796 "No Pole" Half Cents	Very Fine	$ 1,250.00	$ 15,000.00	$ 75,000.00
63	1874 Bickford Ten Dollar	Choice Proof	$ 3,500.00	$ 100,000.00	$ 350,000.00
64	1861-D Gold Dollar	Uncirculated	$ 2,000.00	$ 15,000.00	$ 35,000.00
65	1916-D Mercury Dime	Choice Uncirculated	$ 750.00	$ 3,500.00	$ 10,000.00
66	1895 Morgan Dollar	Choice Proof	$ 1,500.00	$ 17,500.00	$ 25,000.00
67	1796 "No Stars" Quarter Eagle	About Uncirculated	$ 2,500.00	$ 20,000.00	$ 75,000.00
68	1797 Bust Half Dollar	Extremely Fine	$ 2,000.00	$ 15,000.00	$ 45,000.00
69	1836 Gobrecht Dollar	Choice Proof	$ 1,750.00	$ 5,500.00	$ 15,000.00
69	1838 Gobrecht Dollar	Choice Proof	$ 2,500.00	$ 7,500.00	$ 40,000.00
69	1839 Gobrecht Dollar	Choice Proof	$ 2,500.00	$ 7,500.00	$ 40,000.00
70	1795 "Nine Leaves" Ten Dollar	About Uncirculated	$ 1,000.00	$ 12,500.00	$ 75,000.00
71	1796 Bust Quarter	Extremely Fine	$ 1,250.00	$ 7,500.00	$ 17,500.00
72	1796 "15 Stars" Bust Half Dollars	Extremely Fine	$ 2,000.00	$ 15,000.00	$ 45,000.00
72	1796 "16 Stars" Bust Half Dollars	Extremely Fine	$ 2,000.00	$ 16,500.00	$ 50,000.00
73	1854 Gold Dollar Proof Type Two	Choice Proof	$ 3,500.00	$ 35,000.00	$ 150,000.00
73	1855 Gold Dollar Proof Type Two	Choice Proof	$ 3,500.00	$ 35,000.00	$ 125,000.00
74	1870-CC Double Eagle	Extremely Fine	$ 2,500.00	$ 25,000.00	$ 125,000.00
75	1857-S Double Eagle	Choice Uncirculated	$ 250.00	$ 3,500.00	$ 8,500.00
76	1794 "Starred Reverse" Large Cent	Very Fine	$ 1,500.00	$ 10,000.00	$ 75,000.00
77	1864 "Small Motto" Two Cent Proof	Choice Proof	$ 1,500.00	$ 5,000.00	$ 35,000.00
78	1867 "With Rays" Shield Nickel Proof	Choice Proof	$ 1,500.00	$ 5,000.00	$ 45,000.00
79	1827 Bust Quarter Original	Choice Proof	$ 7,000.00	$ 40,000.00	$ 100,000.00
80	1801 Bust Dollar Proof	Choice Proof	$ 4,500.00	$ 35,000.00	$ 150,000.00
80	1802 Bust Dollar Proof	Choice Proof	$ 4,500.00	$ 35,000.00	$ 150,000.00
80	1803 Bust Dollar Proof	Choice Proof	$ 4,500.00	$ 35,000.00	$ 150,000.00
81	1851 Seated Dollar	Choice Proof	$ 1,500.00	$ 7,500.00	$ 37,500.00
82	1852 Seated Dollar	Choice Proof	$ 1,500.00	$ 7,500.00	$ 35,000.00
83	1893-S Morgan Dollar	Choice Uncirculated	$ 2,500.00	$ 35,000.00	$ 125,000.00
84	1870-S Seated Dollar	Extremely Fine	$ 15,000.00	$ 75,000.00	$ 200,000.00
85	1804 "13 Stars" Quarter Eagle	Extremely Fine	$ 2,500.00	$ 7,500.00	$ 75,000.00
86	1841 Quarter Eagle	Extremely Fine	$ 3,500.00	$ 20,000.00	$ 75,000.00
87	1854-S Quarter Eagle	Very Fine	$ 1,500.00	$ 15,000.00	$ 75,000.00
88	1863 Quarter Eagle	Choice Proof	$ 1,500.00	$ 15,000.00	$ 40,000.00
89	1797 "16 Stars" Half Eagle	Extremely Fine	$ 2,500.00	$ 50,000.00	$ 300,000.00
90	1819 Half Eagle	About Uncirculated	$ 1,500.00	$ 25,000.00	$ 45,000.00
90	1819 5D over 50 Half Eagle	About Uncirculated	$ 1,500.00	$ 25,000.00	$ 35,000.00
91	1825/4 Half Eagle	About Uncirculated	$ 2,500.00	$ 125,000.00	$ 250,000.00
92	1832 "12 Stars" Half Eagle	Extremely Fine	$ 3,500.00	$ 45,000.00	$ 125,000.00
93	1875 Half Eagle	About Uncirculated	$ 750.00	$ 25,000.00	$ 75,000.00
94	1798/7 Ten Dollar (9x4 Stars)	About Uncirculated	$ 1,000.00	$ 12,500.00	$ 35,000.00
94	1798/7 Ten Dollar (7x6 Stars)	About Uncirculated	$ 2,500.00	$ 25,000.00	$ 95,000.00
95	1808 Quarter Eagle	About Uncirculated	$ 2,000.00	$ 17,500.00	$ 35,000.00
96	1875 Ten Dollar	About Uncirculated	$ 750.00	$ 20,000.00	$ 80,000.00
97	1854-O Double Eagle	Extremely Fine	$ 500.00	$ 35,000.00	$ 75,000.00
98	1856-O Double Eagle	Extremely Fine	$ 500.00	$ 35,000.00	$ 85,000.00
99	1861-S "Paquet" Double Eagle	About Uncirculated	$ 1,500.00	$ 7,500.00	$ 35,000.00
100	1879 Schoolgirl Dollar	Choice Proof	$ 1,000.00	$ 25,000.00	$ 75,000.00
100	1879 Quintuple Stella	Choice Proof	$ 4,000.00	$ 100,000.00	$ 350,000.00
100	1882 Earring Dollar	Choice Proof	$ 1,000.00	$ 25,000.00	$ 75,000.00

| | **TOTALS** | | * $ 842,250.00 | ** $ 11,197,750.00 | $ 67,040,000.00 |

H.E. Harris & Co. does not buy or sell coins; the historical values shown here reflect our authors' combined 55+ years of dealer experience, their research into auction records, and their review of current auction catalogs. These values are not meant to predict future trends and cannot guarantee future profitability.

* Price does not include: 1870-S Half Dime, 1851-O Seated Dollar

** Price does not include: 1851-O Seated Dollar

DATE/VARIETY	DEN	GRADE	PRICE	DATE	FIRM
1933	G20$	MS65	$ 7,590,020	Jul-02	Sotheby's/Stacks
1804 Original	S$1	PCGS PR68	$ 4,140,000	Aug-99	Bowers & Merena
1804 Original	S$1	PCGS PR64	$ 1,840,000	Oct-00	Stack's
1913 Liberty	5C	NGC PR66	$ 1,840,000	Mar-01	Superior
1804 Original	S$1	PR63	$ 1,815,000	Apr-97	Bowers & Merena
1913 Liberty	5C	GEM PR66	$ 1,485,000	May-96	Bowers & Merena
1907 EX-HR Lt Edg PR	G$20	PCGS PR67	$ 1,210,000	May-99	Ira & Larry Goldberg
1885 Trade	T$1	PR65	$ 907,500	Apr-97	Bowers & Merena
1804 Restrike PR	S$1	PCGS PR58	$ 874,000	Nov-01	Bowers & Merena
1907 EX-HR Lt Edg PR	G$20	PR	$ 825,000	Dec-96	Sotheby's
1839 Type of 38 PR	G$10	NGC PR67	$ 690,000	Sep-99	Ira & Larry Goldberg
1907 EX-HR Lt Edg PR	G$20	PCGS PR67	$ 660,000	Jan-97	Bowers & Merena
1873-CC No Arrows	10C	PCGS MS64	$ 632,500	Apr-99	Heritage
1796 No Stars	G$2.5	BU	$ 605,000	Nov-95	Stack's/RARCOA/Akers
1794	S$1	GEM BU	$ 577,500	Nov-95	Stack's/RARCOA/David Akers
1927-D	G$20	PCGS MS65	$ 577,500	May-98	David Akers
1873-CC No Arrows	10C	MS65	$ 550,000	May-96	Bowers & Merena
1838 PR	G$10	PR	$ 550,000	May-98	David Akers
1889-CC	S$1	PCGS MS68	$ 529,000	Jan-01	Bowers & Merena
1927-D	G$20	GEM BU	$ 522,500	Mar-91	Stack's
1797	50C	GEM BU	$ 517,000	Nov-95	Stack's/RARCOA/David Akers
1884 Trade	T$1	PCGS PR67	$ 510,600	Oct-00	Ira & Larry Goldberg
1833 Large Date PR	G$5	GEM PR	$ 467,500	Oct-97	David Akers
1870-S	S$1	UNC	$ 462,000	Mar-95	Stack's
1889-CC	S$1	MS66PL	$ 462,000	Apr-97	Bowers & Merena
1796 16 Stars	50C	BU	$ 460,000	May-99	Stack's
1894-S	10C	PR64	$ 451,000	May-96	Bowers & Merena
1880 Coil Hair PR	G$4	PCGS PR66	$ 440,000	Aug-91	Superior
Humbert 1852/1	$20	NGC PR64	$ 434,500	Oct-90	Superior
1894-S	10C	GEM PR	$ 431,250	Oct-00	Stack's
1893-S	S$1	SUPERB GEM BU	$ 414,000	Nov-01	Stack's
J-1 1792 Silver Center Cent	P1C	BU	$ 414,000	Jan-02	Stack's
J-452 Transitional 1865 Gold	$20	PCGS PR64	$ 400,000	Aug-90	David Akers/Stack's/RARCOA/Superior
1884 Trade	T$1	PR66	$ 396,000	Apr-97	Bowers & Merena
1857 PR	G$10	NGC PR66	$ 396,000	May-99	Ira & Larry Goldberg
1927-D	G$20	NGC MS66	$ 390,500	Jun-95	Heritage
Humbert 1852/1	$20	PCGS PR65	$ 374,000	May-92	Superior
1829 Small Size	G$5	MS	$ 374,000	Oct-96	Spink America
1909-O	G$5	GEM UNC	$ 374,000	May-98	David Akers
1880 Coil Hair PR	G$4	NGC PR65	$ 368,000	Oct-00	Stack's
J.H. Bowie	$5	PCGS AU58	$ 353,000	Jan-01	Stack's
1796 16 Stars	50C	GEM BU	$ 330,000	Nov-95	Stack's/RARCOA/David Akers
1879 Coil Hair PR	G$4	NGC PR66	$ 310,500	Oct-00	Stack's
1795 Center Bust	S$1	MS67	$ 308,000	Apr-97	Bowers & Merena
1792	H10C	GEM UNC	$ 308,000	Oct-97	David Akers
1880 Coil Hair PR	G$4	PR	$ 308,000	Oct-95	Stack's
1835 PR	G$5	GEM PR	$ 308,000	Oct-97	David Akers
1869 PR	G$20	NGC PR65	$ 308,000	May-90	Superior
1796 No Stars	G$2.5	BU	$ 299,000	May-99	Stack's
1832 12 Stars	G$5	MS	$ 297,000	Oct-96	Spink America
1798 Close Date	G$2.5	PCGS MS65	$ 291,500	Aug-91	Superior
1794	50C	PCGS MS63	$ 288,500	Jan-99	Bowers & Merena
1866 PR	G$2.5	PCGS PR66	$ 275,000	Jul-96	RARCOA/David Akers
1798 Sm Eagle	G$5	PCGS EF40	$ 275,000	May-99	Ira & Larry Goldberg
1798 Close Date	G$2.5	PCGS MS65	$ 268,500	Jun-00	Sotheby's
1884 Trade	S$1	PCGS PR65	$ 264,500	Oct-00	Superior
1880 Coil Hair PR	G$4	PR	$ 264,500	Mar-99	Stack's
1798 Sm Eagle	G$5	PCGS EF40	$ 264,500	Jun-00	Ira & Larry Goldberg
1870-S	S$1	EF45/AU50	$ 264,000	Apr-97	Bowers & Merena
1880 Coil Hair PR	G$4	PR	$ 264,000	Feb-92	Superior
1835 PR	G$5	PR	$ 264,000	May-98	David Akers
1894-S	G$5	NGC MS69	$ 264,000	Aug-90	David Akers
1933	G$10	Very CH UNC	$ 264,000	May-98	David Akers
1895-O	S$1	MS66/67	$ 253,000	Apr-97	Bowers & Merena
1880 Coil Hair PR	G$4	NGC PR64	$ 253,000	Jan-00	Bowers & Merena
1839/8 Type of 1838	G$10	MS65	$ 253,000	Feb-98	Superior

DATE/VARIETY	DEN	GRADE	PRICE	DATE	FIRM
1908 Motto PR	G$20	PR	$ 253,000	Dec-97	Sotheby's
1922 Matte (Low Relief)	S$1	NGC PR64	$ 242,000	Jan-95	Superior
1794	S$1	AU58	$ 241,500	May-99	Bowers & Merena
1825/4	G$5	NGC AU50	$ 241,500	Feb-99	Superior
1829 Large Size	G$5	PCGS MS65	$ 241,500	Oct-99	Bowers & Merena
1796 Stars	G$2.5	AU	$ 231,000	Oct-96	Spink America
1880 Flow Hair PR	G$4	NGC PR65	$ 231,000	Nov-90	Bowers & Merena
1879 Coil Hair PR	G$4	PCGS PR65	$ 231,000	Jul-97	Bowers & Merena
1795 Sm Eagle	G$5	NGC MS65	$ 230,000	Mar-00	Superior
1832	50C	PR65	$ 225,500	Apr-97	Bowers & Merena
1879 Coil Hair PR	G$4	PR	$ 222,000	Oct-95	Stack's
J-1643 1879 Gold	E$20	PR62/63	$ 214,500	May-96	Bowers & Merena
J-1566 1878 Gold	P$2 1/2	PCGS PR65	$ 210,000	Aug-90	David Akers/Stack's/RARCOA/Superior
J-1581 1878 Gold	P$10	PCGS PR64	$ 210,000	Aug-90	David Akers/Stack's/RARCOA/Superior
1817/4	50C	EF45	$ 209,000	Apr-97	Bowers & Merena
1873-CC No Arrows	25C	PCGS MS64	$ 209,000	Feb-98	Superior
1829 Large Size	G$5	PCGS MS64	$ 209,000	Jan-96	Superior
1866 Motto PR	G$5	PR	$ 209,000	Oct-96	Spink America
1925-S	G$20	GEM UNC	$ 209,000	May-98	David Akers
1794	S$1	NGC MS61	$ 207,000	Nov-01	Bowers & Merena
1652 Willow Tree N.2-A, Cr 2-A	Shilng	EF	$ 207,000	Jan-02	Stack's
1795 Sm Eagle	G$5	NGC MS65	$ 207,000	Sep-99	Ira & Larry Goldberg
1933	G$10	PCGS MS65	$ 207,000	Jun-00	Heritage
1856-O	G$20	PCGS MS63	$ 203,500	Jan-95	Superior
1862 PR	G$20	GEM PR	$ 203,500	May-98	David Akers
1921 Special Striking	G$20	PR (Special Striking)	$ 203,500	Jun-00	Sotheby's
1893-S	S$1	MS65/67	$ 198,000	Apr-97	Bowers & Merena
1879 Coil Hair PR	G$4	PR	$ 198,000	Feb-92	Superior
1836 PR	G$5	GEM PR	$ 198,000	Oct-97	David Akers
1822 25/50C	25C	PR65	$ 192,500	Apr-97	Bowers & Merena
1895-O	S$1	PCGS MS65DMPL	$ 189,750	May-01	Heritage
1798/7 7X6 Stars	G$10	PCGS MS61	$ 189,750	Feb-99	Superior
Humbert RE 1852 887	$50RE	NGC MS64	$ 189,500	Jan-99	Bowers & Merena
1870-CC	25C	MS64	$ 187,000	Apr-97	Bowers & Merena
1873-CC No Arrows	25C	MS62	$ 187,000	Apr-97	Bowers & Merena
1933	G$10	PCGS MS64	$ 187,000	Jan-96	Superior
1875 PR	G$20	NGC PR64	$ 187,000	Aug-90	David Akers
1924-S	G$20	GEM UNC	$ 187,000	May-98	David Akers
1817/4	50C	PCGS AU50	$ 184,000	Feb-99	Superior
1828/7	G$5	NGC MS64	$ 184,000	Feb-99	Superior
1904 PR	G$20	PR63	$ 181,500	May-94	Bowers & Merena
1927-S	G$20	NGC MS67	$ 181,500	Jun-95	Heritage
1909-O	G$5	NGC MS65	$ 178,500	Nov-98	Bowers & Merena
1795 9 Leaves	G$10	PCGS MS61	$ 178,500	Mar-98	Heritage
1797 10X6 Stars	S$1	NGC MS65	$ 178,250	Nov-01	Bowers & Merena
1796 No Stars	G$2.5	NGC MS63	$ 178,250	Mar-00	Superior
1841 PR	G$2.5	PCGS PR64	$ 178,250	May-00	Bowers & Merena
1864-S	G$5	PCGS MS65	$ 178,250	Oct-99	Bowers & Merena
1797	50C	GEM UNC	$ 176,000	Oct-96	Spink America
1796	25C	MS65	$ 176,000	Apr-97	Bowers & Merena
1797 10X6 Stars	S$1	MS63	$ 176,000	Apr-97	Bowers & Merena
1893-O	S$1	MS66PL	$ 176,000	Apr-97	Bowers & Merena
1852	25C	GEM PR	$ 176,000	May-98	David Akers
1854 Type 2 PR	G$1	PCGS PR65 (4815783)	$ 176,000	Oct-97	David Akers
1834 Classic PR	G$2.5	PR	$ 176,000	May-98	David Akers
1835 PR	G$2.5	PR	$ 176,000	May-98	David Akers
1848 PR	G$10	PR	$ 176,000	May-98	David Akers
1907 Wire Edge	G$10	GEM UNC	$ 176,000	May-98	David Akers
1875 PR	G$3	NGC PR64	$ 174,900	Aug-90	David Akers
1793 Wreath Vine and Bars	1C	PCGS MS69BN	$ 172,500	Mar-01	Superior
N England N.II-A, Cr ill	Shilng	EF	$ 172,500	Jan-02	Stack's
1652 Willow Tree N.3-D, Cr 3-D	Shilng	EF	$ 172,500	Jan-02	Stack's
Wass Mol 1855	$50	BU	$ 170,500	Dec-96	Sotheby's
1861	G$20	GEM BU	$ 170,500	Aug-90	RARCOA
1793 Chain AMERI. S-1 B-1	1C	AU50	$ 166,750	Jan-02	Stack's
1891 PR	G$20	PCGS PR67	$ 166,750	Oct-99	Bowers & Merena
1807	25C	MS65	$ 165,000	Apr-97	Bowers & Merena
1871-CC	25C	MS65	$ 165,000	Apr-97	Bowers & Merena
1802 Narrow Date	S$1	MS64	$ 165,000	Apr-97	Bowers & Merena
1815	G$5	NGC MS62	$ 65,000	May-99	Ira & Larry Goldberg

DATE/VARIETY	DEN	GRADE	PRICE	DATE	FIRM
1926-D	G$20	GEM UNC	$ 165,000	May-98	David Akers
1796	10C	BU	$ 161,000	May-99	Stack's
1851 Restrike (over a New Orleans dollar)	S$1	ANACS PR62	$ 161,000	Feb-00	Ira & Larry Goldberg
1876-CC	20C	NGC MS66	$ 161,000	Mar-01	Superior
1795 Silver Plug B-7	S$1	CH AU	$ 161,000	Jan-02	Stack's
1893-S	S$1	PCGS MS64	$ 161,000	Feb-02	Ira & Larry Goldberg
N England N.II-A, Cr ill	Shilng	EF	$ 161,000	Jan-02	Stack's
1837 PR	G$2.5	PCGS PR65	$ 161,000	May-00	Bowers & Merena
1879 Coil Hair PR	G$4	NGC PR63	$ 161,000	Sep-98	Heritage
1803 Sm St Rev	G$10	PCGS MS65	$ 161,000	Sep-99	Ira & Larry Goldberg
1797	50C	CH AU	$ 160,000	Oct-96	Stack's
Humbert RE 1852 887	$50RE	BU	$ 159,500	Dec-96	Sotheby's
1828/7	G$5	NGC MS63	$ 159,500	May-99	Ira & Larry Goldberg
1828/7	G$5	MS	$ 159,500	Oct-96	Spink America
1832 12 Stars	G$5	NGC EF45	$ 159,500	May-98	David Akers
1899 PR	G$10	PCGS PR67	$ 159,500	Jan-90	Superior
1848 CAL.	G$2.5	PCGS MS66	$ 156,500	Aug-98	Bowers & Merena
1913-S	G$5	PCGS MS66	$ 156,500	Jan-99	Bowers & Merena
1918/7-D	5C	NGC MS65	$ 155,250	Apr-02	Heritage
1893-S	S$1	PCGS MS65	$ 154,000	Mar-95	Heritage
1853-O No Arrows	50C	VG8	$ 154,000	Apr-97	Bowers & Merena
J-1373 1874 Gold	P$10	PCGS PR64	$ 154,000	Jul-93	Superior
1848-O	G$10	GEM BU	$ 154,000	Oct-94	Stack's
1918/7-S	25C	PCGS MS64FH	$ 149,500	Jan-00	Heritage
1896-O	S$1	PCGS MS65	$ 149,500	Apr-02	Heritage
Baldwin 'Horseman' 1850	$10	PCGS MS64	$ 149,500	May-00	Bowers & Merena
1804 13 Star Rev	G$2.5	PCGS AU55	$ 149,500	Aug-99	Bowers & Merena
1876-CC	20C	MS65	$ 148,500	Apr-97	Bowers & Merena
1855 PR	G$1	GEM PR	$ 148,500	Feb-92	Superior
1831	G$2.5	PCGS MS66	$ 148,500	Aug-90	David Akers
1860 PR	G$20	PCGS PR64	$ 148,500	May-90	Superior
Wass Mol Large Head	$10	PCGS AU58	$ 145,220	Jun-98	Kingswood
Ormsby	$10	PCGS AU50	$ 145,000	May-99	Ira & Larry Goldberg
1880 Flow Hair PR	G$4	NGC PR65	$ 143,750	Oct-00	Stack's
1796 16 Stars	50C	MS63	$ 143,000	Apr-97	Bowers & Merena
1886-O	S$1	MS64	$ 143,000	Apr-97	Bowers & Merena
1850	25C	GEM PR	$ 143,000	May-98	David Akers
1850	50C	CH PR	$ 143,000	May-98	David Akers
1879 Flow Hair PR	G$4	NGC PR66	$ 143,000	Oct-90	Superior
1839 Type of 1840	G$10	BU	$ 143,000	May-98	David Akers
1875 PR	G$10	NGC PR64	$ 143,000	Aug-90	David Akers
1920-S	G$10	NGC MS65	$ 143,000	Jul-96	RARCOA/David Akers
1907 EX-HR Lt Edg PR	G$20	Impaired PR	$ 143,000	Dec-92	Sotheby's
1796 No Stars	G$2.5	PCGS AU58	$ 141,100	Aug-98	Heritage
1795 Center Bust	S$1	PCGS MS65	$ 140,875	Nov-01	Bowers & Merena
1823/2	25C	NGC PR64	$ 138,000	Feb-99	Superior
1796 15 Stars	50C	BU	$ 138,000	May-99	Stack's
1884 Trade	T$1	PCGS PR63	$ 138,000	Apr-02	Heritage
1864 L on Ribbon Die Pair 3	Sm1C	PCGS PR64RD	$ 138,000	Jun-02	Heritage
1652 Willow Tree N.1A, Cr 1-A	Shilng	EF	$ 138,000	Jan-02	Stack's
1796 No Stars	G$2.5	NGC MS62	$ 138,000	Jan-99	Heritage
1879 Coil Hair PR	G$4	PR	$ 138,000	Mar-99	Stack's
1795 Sm Eagle	G$5	PCGS MS63	$ 138,000	Oct-99	Bowers & Merena
1795 13 Leaves	G$10	PCGS MS64	$ 138,000	Aug-99	Bowers & Merena
1907 HR-Flat Edge	G$20	NGC PR68	$ 138,000	Dec-00	Stack's
1871-CC	S$1	CH BU	$ 137,500	Mar-95	Stack's
1883-S	S$1	MS66DMPL	$ 137,500	Apr-97	Bowers & Merena
1879 Coil Hair PR	G$4	PR63	$ 137,500	Aug-95	Bowers & Merena
1797 Sm Eag 16St	G$5	AU	$ 137,500	Oct-96	Spink America
1828/7	G$5	PCGS AU55	$ 137,500	Jan-96	Superior
1927-D	G$20	PCGS AU58	$ 137,500	Jan-93	Superior
1911-D	G$5	NGC MS65	$ 136,150	Jan-98	Heritage
1854-S	G$2.5	PCGS AU50	$ 135,700	Oct-99	Bowers & Merena
1797 Sm Eagle	G$10	BU	$ 135,125	Jan-00	Stack's
1822 25/50C	25C	NGC PR68	$ 133,400	Mar-00	Superior
1794	S$1	NGC AU55	$ 132,250	Mar-01	Bowers & Merena
1802/1 Wide Date B-3 BB-234	S$1	BU	$ 132,250	Jan-02	Stack's
1880 Flow Hair PR	G$4	GEM PR	$ 132,250	Oct-00	Stack's
1879 Coil Hair PR	G$4	NGC PR63	$ 132,250	Aug-01	Heritage
1892-S	S$1	MS67	$ 132,000	Apr-97	Bowers & Merena

DATE/VARIETY	DEN	GRADE	PRICE	DATE	FIRM
1839 No Drapery	25C	CH PR	$ 132,000	May-98	David Akers
1839 Drapery	50C	CH PR	$ 132,000	May-98	David Akers
1855 PR	G$1	NGC PR65 Cam	$ 132,000	Jan-93	Superior
1846-O	G$2.5	CH BU	$ 132,000	May-98	David Akers
1864	G$2.5	GEM BU	$ 132,000	Oct-96	Spink America
1850 PR	G$2.5	NGC PR62	$ 132,000	Sep-90	Bowers & Merena
1854	G$3	PCGS MS67	$ 132,000	Jan-90	Superior
1820 Curl 2 Lg Let	G$5	BU	$ 132,000	Oct-94	Stack's
1800	G$10	BU	$ 132,000	May-98	David Akers
1907 HR-Flat Edge	G$20	NGC PR65	$ 132,000	May-90	Superior
1927-S	G$20	PCGS MS66	$ 132,000	May-98	David Akers
1796 No Stars	G$2.5	NGC AU58	$ 129,000	Jan-98	Heritage
1916-D	10C	PCGS MS67FB	$ 128,800	Apr-01	Heritage
1806 Pointed 6, Stem	50C	MS65	$ 126,500	Apr-97	Bowers & Merena
1886-O	S$1	PCGS MS65	$ 126,500	Aug-99	Kingswood
1853 Arrows and Rays	50C	NGC PR65	$ 126,500	Feb-02	Ira & Larry Goldberg
1884 Trade	T$1	PR	$ 126,500	Mar-02	Stack's
1879 Flow Hair PR	G$4	PCGS PR66	$ 126,500	Aug-99	Bowers & Merena
1879 Coil Hair PR	G$4	NGC PR62	$ 126,500	Jan-00	Bowers & Merena
1880 Coil Hair PR	G$4	NGC PR61	$ 126,500	Jan-00	Heritage
1795 Sm Eagle	G$5	PCGS MS63	$ 126,500	Aug-00	Bowers & Merena
1875 PR	G$5	NGC PR64	$ 126,500	Aug-90	David Akers
1930-S	G$20	GEM UNC	$ 126,500	May-98	David Akers
1930-S	G$20	GEM BU	$ 126,500	Mar-91	Stack's
1875	T$1	PCGS MS68	$ 125,700	Jul-97	Heritage
1933	G$10	PCGS MS64	$ 123,625	Mar-00	Superior
1796 No Stars	G$2.5	MS61	$ 123,500	Sep-97	Heritage
1921	G$20	NGC MS64	$ 123,500	Jul-97	Heritage
1821	25C	PR66	$ 121,000	Apr-97	Bowers & Merena
1835	50C	PR66	$ 121,000	Apr-97	Bowers & Merena
1838-O	50C	PR60	$ 121,000	Apr-97	Bowers & Merena
1891-CC	S$1	MS66DMPL	$ 121,000	Apr-97	Bowers & Merena
1883-O	S$1	PR66	$ 121,000	Apr-97	Bowers & Merena
1837	25C	GEM PR	$ 121,000	May-98	David Akers
1855 PR	G$1	PCGS PR66 (6556067)	$ 121,000	Oct-97	David Akers
1807 Bust Left	G$5	PCGS MS67	$ 121,000	Nov-99	Sotheby's
1833 Small Date	G$5	NGC MS64	$ 121,000	Aug-90	Superior
1838	G$5	AU (possible Proof)	$ 121,000	Oct-96	Spink America
1876-CC	G$5	NGC MS65	$ 121,000	May-90	Superior
1907 RolledEdge	G$10	GEM UNC	$ 121,000	May-98	David Akers
1907 RolledEdge	G$10	NGC MS65	$ 121,000	Jan-90	Superior
1933	G$10	PCGS MS64	$ 121,000	Jul-96	RARCOA/David Akers
1933	G$10	PCGS MS63	$ 121,000	Aug-90	Superior
1910 PR	G$20	NGC PR67	$ 121,000	Aug-91	MARCA
1896 PR	G$20	GEM PR	$ 121,000	Oct-97	David Akers
1796 15 Stars	50C	MS64	$ 120,750	May-99	Stack's
1839 No Drapery	50C	PCGS PR63	$ 120,750	Feb-01	Ira & Larry Goldberg
1895-O	S$1	NGC MS65DMPL	$ 120,750	Feb-01	Ira & Larry Goldberg
1802	S$1	PCGS PR64	$ 120,750	Nov-01	Bowers & Merena
1919-D	50C	PCGS MS65	$ 120,750	Apr-02	Heritage
1893-S	S$1	NGC MS64	$ 120,750	Apr-02	Heritage
1796/5	G$5	BU	$ 120,750	May-99	Stack's
1845 PR	G$10	PCGS PR64	$ 120,750	Aug-99	Heritage
1870-CC	G$20	PCGS EF45	$ 120,750	Jun-00	Ira & Larry Goldberg
1802/1	G$5	PCGS MS63	$ 119,800	Jan-90	Superior
1909 PR	G$20	PR	$ 118,250	Jun-93	Sotheby's
1833 Small Date	G$5	NGC MS65	$ 118,000	Aug-98	Heritage
1875 PR	G$3	PCGS PR65	$ 117,875	Aug-01	Heritage
1803	S$1	NGC PR65	$ 115,500	Aug-95	Superior
J-1566 1878 Gold	P$2 1/2	PCGS PR65	$ 115,500	Jan-93	Superior
1855 PR	G$1	BR PR	$ 115,500	Oct-92	Stack's
1795 9 Leaves	G$10	NGC MS61	$ 115,500	Sep-90	Christie's
1921	G$20	PCGS MS64	$ 115,500	May-99	Ira & Larry Goldberg
1796 16 Stars	50C	NGC MS64	$ 115,250	Aug-98	Bowers & Merena
1943-S Copper	Sm1C	NGC MS61BN	$ 115,000	Feb-00	Ira & Larry Goldberg
1919-D	10C	PCGS MS66FB	$ 115,000	Oct-00	Heritage
1892-S	S$1	PCGS MS67	$ 115,000	May-01	Heritage
1876-CC	20C	CH BU	$ 115,000	Mar-02	Stack's
1794 B-1 BB-1	S$1	PCGS EF40	$ 115,000	Jun-02	Bowers & Merena
N England N.III-C, Cr I,3	Shilng	CH VF	$ 115,000	Jan-02	Stack's

DATE/VARIETY	DEN	GRADE	PRICE	DATE	FIRM
1943-S Copper	Sm1C	NGC MS61BN	$ 115,000	Feb-00	Ira & Larry Goldberg
1796 Stars	G$2.5	BU	$ 115,000	May-99	Stack's
1796 Stars	G$2.5	BU	$ 115,000	May-99	Stack's
1833	G$2.5	NGC MS67	$ 115,000	Sep-99	Ira & Larry Goldberg
1841 PR	G$2.5	PCGS PR60	$ 115,000	Oct-99	Bowers & Merena
1797 Sm Eag 16St	G$5	PCGS AU55	$ 115,000	Oct-99	Bowers & Merena
1838	G$5	PCGS MS65 (possible Proof)	$ 115,000	Oct-99	Bowers & Merena
1865-S 865/Inv186	G$10	PCGS MS64	$ 115,000	May-99	Bowers & Merena
1842-D Small Date	G$5	NGC MS62	$ 112,750	May-95	Stack's
1892-S	S$1	PCGS MS65	$ 112,700	Feb-02	Ira & Larry Goldberg
1801	H10C	NGC MS67	$ 112,500	Aug-98	Bowers & Merena
Clark Gr 1860	$20	PCGS AU55	$ 112,200	Sep-97	Kingswood
1875 PR	G$20	NGC PR64 DCAM	$ 112,125	Aug-01	Heritage
1796 15 Stars	50C	MS63	$ 110,000	Apr-97	Bowers & Merena
1827	50C	PR65	$ 110,000	Apr-97	Bowers & Merena
1822 25/50C	25C	GEM PR	$ 110,000	May-98	David Akers
1802 Wide Date	S$1	PCGS MS65	$ 110,000	Nov-99	Sotheby's
Kellogg 1855	$50	PCGS PR53	$ 110,000	Aug-90	David Akers/Stack's/RARCOA/Superior
J-1547 1877 Copper	P$50	CH PRBN	$ 110,000	Oct-97	David Akers
1836 PR	G$2.5	PR	$ 110,000	May-98	David Akers
1875 PR	G$3	NGC PR64	$ 110,000	Feb-91	Superior
1880 Flow Hair PR	G$4	NGC PR65	$ 110,000	Jun-00	Sotheby's
1847	G$5	GEM UNC	$ 110,000	Oct-97	David Akers
1913-S	G$5	GEM UNC	$ 110,000	May-98	David Akers
1875 PR	G$20	PR	$ 110,000	Jun-95	Sotheby's
1897-O	S$1	PCGS MS67	$ 109,250	Jan-01	Heritage
J-10 1792 Copper	P10C	PCGS EF45	$ 109,250	Feb-01	Ira & Larry Goldberg
1803 Sm St Rev	G$10	PCGS MS65	$ 109,250	Mar-00	Superior
1921	G$20	PCGS MS64	$ 109,250	Sep-99	Ira & Larry Goldberg
1873-CC No Arrows	25C	PCGS MS62	$ 106,375	Apr-99	Heritage
1856-O	G$20	PCGS AU53	$ 105,800	Oct-99	Bowers & Merena
1803/2	G$5	PCGS MS66	$ 105,600	Feb-99	Kingswood
1825/4	G$5	AU50	$ 105,600	Sep-92	Bowers & Merena
1883 PR	G$20	PCGS PR65	$ 104,650	Aug-99	Kingswood
1838-O	50C	PCGS PR63	$ 104,500	Jan-96	Bowers & Merena
1864-S	25C	MS66	$ 104,500	Apr-97	Bowers & Merena
1797	50C	MS60	$ 104,500	Apr-97	Bowers & Merena
1797 15 Stars	H10C	GEM UNC	$ 104,500	Oct-97	David Akers
1833	G$2.5	BU	$ 104,500	Oct-94	Stack's
1795 Lg Eagle	G$5	BU	$ 104,500	Oct-94	Stack's
1831	G$5	PCGS MS65	$ 104,500	May-91	Superior
1859-C	G$5	NGC MS66	$ 104,500	May-95	Stack's
1863	G$10	NGC MS63	$ 104,500	Aug-91	MARCA
1796 Small Date, Lg Let	S$1	BU	$ 103,500	May-99	Stack's
1918/7-D	5C	PCGS MS64	$ 103,500	Aug-00	Bowers & Merena
1895	S$1	NGC PR68	$ 103,500	Apr-02	Heritage
1793 Wreath Vine and Bars	1C	PCGS MS66RB	$ 103,500	Nov-01	Heritage
Assay 900	$20	PR63	$ 103,500	May-99	Bowers & Merena
J-7 1792 Silver	H10C	PCGS AU58	$ 103,500	Jan-02	Bowers & Merena
1796 No Stars	G$2.5	NGC MS62	$ 103,500	Mar-00	Superior
1880 Flow Hair PR	G$4	PCGS PR64	$ 103,500	Sep-98	Heritage
1796/5	G$5	BU	$ 103,500	May-99	Stack's
1815	G$5	PCGS AU58	$ 103,500	Oct-99	Bowers & Merena
1797 Sm Eagle	G$10	PCGS AU58	$ 103,500	Oct-99	Bowers & Merena
1854-O	G$20	PCGS AU55	$ 103,500	May-00	Bowers & Merena
1818	50C	PR65	$ 103,400	Apr-97	Bowers & Merena
1879 Flow Hair PR	G$4	PCGS PR66	$ 103,400	Nov-99	Sotheby's
1907 Rolled Edge	G$10	PCGS MS66	$ 101,775	Feb-00	Superior
1846 PR	G$10	PR63	$ 101,750	Aug-90	David Akers
1805/4	50C	NGC MS65	$ 101,500	Aug-98	Heritage
1871-CC	S$1	PCGS MS63	$ 101,500	Sep-98	Bowers & Merena
1885 PR	G$20	NGC PR66	$ 101,500	Aug-98	Heritage
1880 Flow Hair PR	G$4	NGC PR64	$ 101,200	Aug-96	Heritage
1927-S	25C	PCGS MS65FH	$ 100,625	Mar-00	Superior
1850-O	G$10	PCGS MS65	$ 100,625	May-99	Superior
1827	G$5	PCGS MS65	$ 100,100	Sep-97	Superior
J-661 1868 Gold	P$10	PCGS PR63	$ 100,000	Aug-90	David Akers/Stack's/RARCOA/Superior
1867	G$3	PCGS MS67	$ 100,000	May-90	Superior

BIBLIOGRAPHY

Akers, David W. *United States Gold Coins; An Analysis of Auction Records, Volume I: Gold Dollars*. Englewood, Ohio: Paramount Publications, 1975.

Akers, David W. *United States Gold Coins; An Analysis of Auction Records, Volume II: Quarter Eagles*. Englewood, Ohio: Paramount Publications, 1975.

Akers, David W. *United States Gold Coins; An Analysis of Auction Records, Volume III: Three Dollar Gold*. Englewood, Ohio: Paramount Publications, 1976.

Akers, David W. *United States Gold Coins; An Analysis of Auction Records, Volume IV: Half Eagles*. Englewood, Ohio: Paramount Publications, 1979.

Akers, David W. *United States Gold Coins; An Analysis of Auction Records, Volume V: Eagles*. Englewood, Ohio: Paramount Publications, 1980.

Akers, David W. *United States Gold Coins; An Analysis of Auction Records, Volume VI: Double Eagles*. Englewood, Ohio: Paramount Publications, 1982.

Akers, David W. *United States Gold Patterns*. Englewood, Ohio: Paramount Publications, 1975.

Breen, Walter. *Walter Breen's Encyclopedia of United States and Colonial Proof Coins, 1722-1977*. New York, New York: FCI Press, Inc., 1977.

Breen, Walter. *Walter Breen's Complete Encyclopedia of United States and Colonial Coins*. New York, New York: Doubleday, 1988.

Bowers, Q. *David. United States Gold Coins, An Illustrated History*. Wolfeboro, New Hampshire: Bowers and Merena Galleries, 1982.

CoinFacts.com. CoinFacts.com, Inc. <http://www.coinfacts.com/>

Dannreuther, John & Garrett, Jeff. *United States Small Cents – Silver Dollar: Significant Auction Records 1995-June 2000*. Newport Beach, California: Collectors Universe, 2000.

Dannreuther, John & Garrett, Jeff. *United States Small Cents – Silver Dollar: Significant Auction Records 1997-March 2002*. Newport Beach, California: Collectors Universe, 2002.

Guth, Ron. *Coin Collecting For Dummies*. New York, New York: Hungry Minds, 2001.

Logan, Russell & McCloskey, John W. *Federal Half Dimes 1792-1837*. Manchester, Michigan: John Reich Collectors Society, 1998.

Pollock III, Andrew W. *United States Patterns and Related Issues*. Wolfeboro, New Hampshire: Bowers and Merena Galleries, 1994

The PCGS Population Report, October 2002. Newport Beach, California: The Professional Coin Grading Service.

Winter, Douglas and Cutler, Lawrence E. *Gold Coins of the Old West, The Carson City Mint 1870-1893*. Wolfeboro, New Hampshire: Bowers and Merena Galleries, 1994.

Winter, Douglas. *New Orleans Mint Gold Coins 1839-1909*. Wolfeboro, New Hampshire: Bowers and Merena Galleries, 1992.

Various Auction Catalogs from:

Auctions by Bowers and Merena

Bowers and Merena Galleries

Heritage Numismatic Auctions, Inc.

Ira and Larry Goldberg Coins & Collectibles, Inc.

Mid-American Rare Coin Auctions, Inc.

Paramount Rare Coins

Sotheby's

Stack's

Superior Galleries